HOW TO IMPROVE YOUR SELF-ESTEEM

HOW TO IMPROVE YOUR SELF-ESTEEM

Elaine Sheehan

COLLINS & BROWN

Copyright © Vega 2002
Text copyright © Elaine Sheehan 2002

First published in 2002 by Vega
This issue published in 2007 by
Collins & Brown
151 Freston Road
London
W10 6TH

An imprint of Anova Books Company Ltd

Distributed in the United States and Canada by
Sterling Publishing Co, 387 Park Avenue South, New York, NY 10016, USA

ISBN: 9 78184 340 410 1

A CIP catalogue record for this book is available from the British Library.

10 9 8 7 6 5 4 3 2 1

Printed and bound by Creative Print and Design, Ebbw Vale, Wales

This book can be ordered direct from the publisher.
Contact the marketing department, but try your bookshop first.

www.anovabooks.com

Contents

To Luke

Know that you are forever loved

Illustrations

Acknowledgements

I am grateful to my teachers and particularly my clients, past and present, who are an invaluable source of further learning. Special thanks are due to those who allowed me to include them in this work (false names have been used to protect their identities). I would also like to acknowledge my debt to my husband Mark, my father Paddy and my brother Trevor for their continued support and enthusiasm.

Introduction

There is but one cause of human failure and that is man's lack of faith in his true self.

WILLIAM JAMES[1]

To have healthy self-esteem is a fundamental human yearning and something we constantly strive for. However, some people never achieve a self-image they can feel comfortable with, living their lives forever tormented by doubts about themselves. This book is about the way we view ourselves and addresses those issues which contribute to the development and maintenance of this self-perception. More importantly, it brings together some of the most useful techniques for creating and enhancing self-esteem that I have come across in my personal and professional study of this fascinating subject. If you wish to make a personal journey of self-exploration and growth which aims to push forward your boundaries of self-understanding and insight and, above all, to bring about positive change, then this book is definitely for you!

The best investment you will ever make in your life is to take time to work on improving your self-esteem. Low self-esteem can cause us to hide our true selves in shame. We put up defensive facades and firmly place a lid on our potential. This book is about helping you to stop hiding from yourself and others. It is about mastering your life rather than being a victim. It is about self-acceptance and self-love. It is about *you*. Follow your dreams. Make your future the very best it can be. Turn this page in your life!

CHAPTER 1

Exploring the Concept of Self-Esteem

The self-concept can . . .be a complete misconception.

REX JOHNSON AND DAVID SWINDLEY[1]

WHAT IS SELF-ESTEEM?

Sarah comes across as very confident and comfortable in herself. She makes the most of her talents and is enthusiastic about life. She has a positive view of what she has to offer the world and commands a healthy respect from those around her. She feels she is worthy of love, happiness and fulfilling relationships. In contrast, Ellen believes she is useless and has trouble accepting that she is in any way lovable. She constantly finds herself in relationships where she is badly treated. She does not feel she deserves any better. She finds it hard to see anything positive in her future. In comparing these two individuals we might say that Sarah has high self-esteem while Ellen has low self-esteem. Some of us might recognize ourselves in Sarah or Ellen, though many of us probably fluctuate somewhere in between the two. But what is 'self-esteem'?

Self-esteem can be viewed as the degree to which we value ourselves. Research suggests that our awareness or concept of self is thought to arise mainly out of our social experiences. We come to see ourselves as we perceive others see us. Almost a century ago the sociologist Cooley wrote in a poetic style how our view of ourselves is like a mirror which reflects the imagined evaluations of others about us: 'Each to each a looking glass, reflects the other that doth pass.'[2] Therefore, the self-concept which incorporates the notion of self-esteem appears to be formed and developed from the outside inwards. Particularly in our early years, we are dramatically influenced by what other people think about us. This colours our view of ourselves. It is interesting to appreciate that if we had been brought up in a different way we might now have a different self-esteem, even though we are still essentially the same person.

WHAT CAUSES LOW SELF-ESTEEM?

As I look into the eyes of my one-year-old child I see complete ease and happiness. I remember once seeing printed on a baby bib the following: 'I love my mommy, I love my daddy, I just love everybody!' The message could have also included: 'I love myself.' Babies think everything and everybody in life is wonderful – including themselves. They feel happy to be who they are and do not feel the need to pretend to be anyone else. Each day they busily get on with enjoying their lives. The initial tendency to feel good about ourselves and the world around us is something we are all born with. However, over time, as our concept of self develops, this natural bias is challenged and threatened in a variety of ways. Researchers have examined many variables in this respect, including upbringing, physical or sexual abuse, trauma, physical appearance, gender and current life events.

Upbringing

The last section emphasized the importance of other people in terms of their effect on the development of our view of ourselves. In particular the quality of the relationships experienced in childhood appears to be vitally important, since it is at this time that the seeds of self-esteem are sown. A child's mother (or primary caretaker) is thought to play a central role in this respect. If the mother-child relationship is healthy (that is, if the child perceives the mother as responsive and sensitive), then the child can develop a positive sense of self and the ability to form close personal relationships in adulthood. The opposite is thought to hold true if the mother-child relationship is poor. Failure to form an affectionate attachment to the mother can result in perpetual anxiety regarding abandonment or rejection.

The messages children receive about themselves from significant people around them as they grow are very important to their self-esteem. Children tend to accept things at face value. Indeed, this is what can often add to their charm. I remember seeing a father teaching his little son how to use his toy golf club. As he held the club in an arc over his head his father advised, 'Keep your eye on the ball.' On hearing this, much to the amusement of the onlookers, the child bent down and physically placed his eye on the ball! This really highlights the simplistic logic of a child's mind. Everything is taken literally. If a significant person in a child's life is regularly saying negative or hurtful things about that child, the content of these comments will be taken on board to the detriment of that child's self-esteem. It does not matter if this person also shows love to this child and 'does not really mean' these comments but was just having a bad day or only intending to 'playfully tease' the child. Children need very clear, straightforward and consistent messages letting them know that they are loved and worthwhile.

Parents' own self-esteem may also have an effect on their children. It is thought that the degree to which parents have worked on their own issues of personal self-esteem will have a greater effect on their children than anything they might attempt to teach them directly. As children we initially learn how to treat ourselves by copying our parents' behaviour. Therefore, if a parent is very critical of us, we become self-critical. Ellen's father never praised her if she did something well, but would shout abuse at her if she did something in a manner unacceptable to him. As an adult, Ellen carried on this legacy in her mind – never acknowledging things she did well and criticizing herself mercilessly if she felt she was performing below what she expected of herself.

Finally, family functioning and structure are thought to be important to self-esteem. Studies have found that children of divorced parents and the homeless can develop a lower view of themselves as a result of their circumstances. Also, if there is illness or alcohol abuse within the family, self-esteem can be adversely affected. As a child, Thomas never knew what to expect when he arrived home from school. Most of the time his mother would be sober and a meal would have been prepared. However, there were periods when he would regularly find her slumped in a chair with an empty bottle of vodka nearby. On one occasion, Thomas came home to find his mother uncon-scious in the shower – she had passed out and hit her head. For one terrifying moment he thought she was dead. Since his father worked long hours, Thomas took it on himself to adopt the role of 'caretaker' from that day onwards. He was afraid that something terrible might happen to his mother if he did not watch out for her. He had been told that his mother's drinking was a 'secret' and so he did not feel he could ask anyone for help. This whole situation was to the detriment of Thomas's own emotional needs and as an adult he reported feeling 'needy' and insecure.

Physical or sexual abuse

'Spare the rod and spoil the child' is often the justification given for physical abuse of children. Such abuse is often random and unpredictable, resulting over time in feelings of complete helplessness in victims. Being threatened with or suffering physical violence can severely affect self-esteem.

The effects of sexual abuse in childhood also reverberate throughout the life of the sufferer. Derek Jehu speaks of the self-denigrating beliefs associated with childhood sexual abuse that contribute to low self-esteem.[3] Victims of such abuse often believe that they are 'worthless or bad' and 'inferior to other people'. Gael Lindenfield, in her book simply entitled *Self-Esteem*,[4] notes how being subjected to inappropriate sexual innuendo can also serve to threaten the development of a positive self-concept.

Trauma

Traumatic experiences can ultimately leave their mark on a person's self-esteem. For instance, I remember a client who had witnessed a horrific car accident a number of years before coming to see me. The memory of this event continued to haunt him, causing him to feel edgy and anxious much of the time. He suffered from panic attacks and was finding it increasingly difficult to function effectively in life. This in turn had eroded his confidence.

Similarly, another client suffering from claustrophobia and panic attacks recounted to me the traumatic memory of being in hospital to have her tonsils out when she was seven years old. The old way of anaesthetizing patients – by putting a mask over the mouth for the inhalation of ether – was a *terrifying* experience for that small child. She remembered the room where it had happened, with cream-coloured tiles and pipes running along the wall. She reported that it reminded her of a bathroom. Also this room had no windows. As an adult she found it impossible to enter any public bathroom without a window. She was finding the more she avoided public bathrooms the more her anxiety developed. Her world became increasingly limited. In time, she began to avoid leaving home, out of fear that she may need to use a bathroom during her period away from her house. She had a very poor view of herself, believing she was 'stupid' to be behaving in a manner which to her seemed 'completely irrational'.

Physical appearance

A quick look through the pages of any popular fashion magazine highlights the great importance society places on 'looking good', no matter what your age. The physical self-concept is thought to be one of the primary building blocks for general self-esteem among children. Those considered attractive receive more positive attention than those who are perceived to have a less pleasing appearance.

Ultimately, as you move into adulthood, it is not how you actually look that matters but rather how you perceive your own appearance. I remember a client revealing to me that she felt ugly and fat. She hated looking at herself in the mirror. Before me sat a tall, slender and elegant woman with a beautiful face. As a child, however, she had been overweight and wore thick-rimmed glasses and braces on her teeth. At home she was constantly reminded that her sister had the good looks and at school she was teased daily. As an adult this woman was finding it difficult to believe anything other than that she was unattractive.

Gender

In the past, despite inconclusive evidence, many authors writing in this area have tended to follow traditional sex stereotyping and assumed that in general females have lower self-esteem than males.[5] More recent research[6] deduces that 'boy and girls tend to be much more similar than different' with respect to how they value themselves.

Current life events

No matter how robust an individual's self-esteem may be, life has the tendency to present experiences that will consistently challenge a positive evaluation of self. Being put down or humiliated by others, receiving a refusal for a job or entry onto a course, being ill or made redundant – all of these experiences can have detrimental consequences for a positive perception of self.

HOW DO YOU VALUE YOURSELF?

How you value yourself is not necessarily indicative of the image you present to other people, nor does it have to match who you truly are. It is purely your own evaluation of yourself – which may be accurate or completely inaccurate. There are hundreds of self-esteem measures available. The measurement presented in figure 1 is adapted from Rosenberg's Self-Esteem Scale,[7] which is one of the most widely used measures of self-esteem in existence.

All self-esteem instruments are problematic in that they rely on a single means of measurement – how individuals decide to present themselves. This can potentially contaminate scores since few people are so uninfluenced by society that the desire to 'look good' in the eyes of others is irrelevant to them. However, this test of your level of self-esteem is purely for your eyes (unless of course you decide to share its result with other people). So, if you do not answer the questions in the scale as honestly as you can, it is only yourself you are fooling.

To find your total score on the scale merely add your scores for the ten statements. For our purposes here it can be taken that a score above 0 indicates a tendency towards high self-esteem, with very high self-esteem receiving a full score of 10. Scoring below 0 signifies an inclination towards low self-esteem, with a score of –10 indicating very low self-esteem. The higher your score the higher your self-esteem, the lower your score the lower your self-esteem.

MEASURING YOUR SELF-ESTEEM

Score the following descriptions on the basis of whether you agree or disagree that they apply to you.

Scoring for statements 1 to 5:
Agree = +1 Disagree = −1

1   I feel I'm a person of worth, at least on an equal basis with others.
2   I feel I have a number of good qualities.
3   I am able to do things as well as most people.
4   I take a positive attitude towards myself.
5   On the whole, I am satisfied with myself.

Scoring for statements 6 to 10:
Agree = −1 Disagree = +1

6   I feel I do not have much to be proud of.
7   All in all, I am inclined to feel that I am a failure.
8   I wish I could have more respect for myself.
9   I certainly feel useless at times.
10 At times I think I am no good at all.

TOTAL SCORE: Add up scores for the ten statements.

Figure 1 *Self-esteem scale*

THE BENEFITS OF HIGH SELF-ESTEEM

In my years of seeing clients who are committed to improving their self-esteem, I have heard first-hand many of the general benefits they begin to notice quite soon after they have begun their work on themselves. I have brought a sample of their comments together in the following list. As you read it, be assured that in time you can have your own similar list, which will incorporate some or maybe even all of these benefits!

- More accepting of myself and others
- Clearer about what I want from life
- More relaxed and in a better position to handle stress
- Much more positive and feeling happier
- Willing to take more responsibility for myself and feeling more in control of life – more independent
- Better at listening to others
- Feeling more 'balanced'
- More comfortable in social situations
- More self-reliant and creative, less bound by the opinions of others
- Improved appearance, more 'radiant'
- More in a position to receive as well as give love
- Gentler with myself; able to take more risks because I now realize there is no such thing as failure, just valuable learning experiences
- Able to congratulate others on their achievements without feelings of jealousy
- More confident in all activities
- 'Problems' become 'challenges'
- More willing to share feelings with others and to be assertive
- Able to talk honestly about shortcomings and achievements
- More excited, motivated and enthusiastic about life.

If you scored high on the self-esteem scale in the last section, it will be important to put in some work to improve things even further (I do not know anyone who would say 'no' to an even healthier self-esteem!), or at the very least to maintain your present positive view of self. If you have scored low on the self-esteem scale it will be even more obvious why working towards changing the way you view yourself will be worthwhile.

CHAPTER 2

Problems Associated with Low Self-Esteem

You are not alone in feeling low self-esteem: nearly everyone does at some time.

PATRICIA CLEGHORN[1]

Most people would agree that having low self-esteem can have a profound effect on the potential for happiness and success in life. In particular, our level of self-esteem can have a powerful influence on the nature of our relationships with others and our psychological health. This chapter highlights why you cannot afford to have low self-esteem. The following areas will be explored in this respect: self-acceptance and acceptance of others; fear of abandonment; perfectionism; use of defence mechanisms; addictions; awareness of feelings, needs and wants; control issues; decision making; initiating communication with others.

SELF-ACCEPTANCE AND ACCEPTANCE OF OTHERS

The American psychologist Carl Rogers noted that the more accepting individuals are of themselves the more likely they are to accept others.[2] Conversely, the lower our opinion of ourselves the less accepting we are of other people. If you have grown up in an environment where you were heavily criticized, you may be inclined to continue to act out this treatment on yourself into adulthood by being critical of yourself rather than being supportive in your everyday thoughts. All too often you may also find yourself being critical of others. This process of criticizing others can actually become addictive. While engaged in judging others and putting them down you are not only temporarily distracted from your negative feelings about yourself, but can also feel 'one up'. In effect, the trend seems to be that we 'do unto ourselves what has been done unto us' as well as 'doing unto others what has been done unto us'. If we have experienced negative influences on our self-concept while growing up, we will continue to inflict negativity not only on ourselves but also on those around us.

FEAR OF ABANDONMENT

I have worked with countless clients who choose to remain in destructive relationships out of a fear of being on their own. Often they put up with appalling conditions but soldier on because they are convinced they 'love' the person they are with. Often they are confusing dependency with love. For example, Cathy as a child did not feel loved and accepted. She found in adulthood that she was sabotaging her relationships with an insatiable craving for love, affection and attention. She was continuously asking her present boyfriend if he loved her. She could never hear it often enough. She reported that if he ever left her she would be 'nothing'. She was depending on him to meet her childhood needs.

PERFECTIONISM

If while growing up we have felt valued for our achievements rather than for who we are, we may find ourselves driven to continuously achieve into adulthood. Unless we are achieving we do not feel worthwhile. And even when we are achieving we can never quite fill the void inside – it is never enough. We are rarely completely happy with what we have managed. When comparing our achievements with those of other people we inevitably look at those who seem to have done better than us and so the comparison usually leaves us feeling worse. In this way we continually perpetuate our feelings of inadequacy.

Perfectionism not only results in increased dissatisfaction with yourself and your achievements, but also can seep into everything else in your life. Maybe you find yourself constantly criticizing your partner in all he or she does because it 'is not good enough', or moving from relationship to relationship in an attempt to find the 'perfect partner'. You may find you work so hard at achieving that you have no real room in your life to be there for anyone else. Perhaps you find life a constant uphill struggle, never having space to rest and just 'be' – you become a human 'doing' rather than a human 'being'.

USE OF DEFENCE MECHANISMS

How can we define reality? Reality is usually whatever we interpret it to be and so in a sense we all create our own reality. Sometimes we distort our perceived reality in such a way so as to protect ourselves from negative feelings. We do this by employing defence mechanisms or strategies to prevent anxiety. Rather than dealing directly with what we experience, we avoid it. Individuals low in self-esteem are prone to engage in defensive and self-protective behaviour and tend to over-utilize psychological defence strategies.

All of us use defences from time to time. In the short term they can buy us space so that we can ease ourselves into adjustment. However, used long term, defence mechanisms can become a regular way of avoiding dealing directly with stressful situations or problems, or, indeed, new information about ourselves. The following are some of the more commonly used defence mechanisms.

Denial

If an external reality feels threatening we may deny its existence. For example, the trauma of the death of a loved one may be too immense for us to take in all at once. We may initially still talk and act as if the person is still alive. Slowly, as we move through the grieving process and are more prepared to deal with the trauma, reality sinks in and denial is replaced by emotions such as anger and sorrow. People with low self-esteem can over-use the defence mechanism of denial when faced with information inconsistent with their negative view of self. For instance, every time a woman with low self-esteem is given a compliment by her husband on her appearance she may deny his words or rationalize them in some other light such as 'He is just saying that to try to make me feel good.' She may do this because such praise contradicts what she believes about herself.

Repression

While denial relates to external reality, repression is a defence against internal threat. It is a subconscious process; the individual will be unaware of whatever has been repressed. For instance, if as a child you felt a lot of hostility and anger towards your mother, these feelings and memories may be repressed to avoid anxiety because the notion that 'you should always love your mother' may be present in your concept of self. Repressing these feelings results in the alienation of part of the self. Often the individual will experience depression.

Projection

If we have certain traits or qualities that we disown or fail to acknowledge, one way to handle them may be to attribute them to others, often in magnified amounts. Like repression, this mechanism is also operated outside of conscious awareness. So, for example, if you are feeling irritable you may find yourself accusing your spouse/partner of being in a 'really bad mood'! Consciously, you will see him or her as having the 'problem'.

Reaction formation

This defence mechanism can be taken on board as added insurance that repressed feelings will be kept out of conscious awareness. It involves giving strong expression to the opposite of the repressed feeling. For instance, if you have repressed a feeling that you are not a very nice person you may behave in a manner that will help you to feel that you are a very nice person. This may involve being 'kind to a fault', imposing yourself in this fashion on others, whether or not it is warranted, just so that you can avoid your true feelings about yourself. Another example of the strategy of reaction formation is when a person who feels unimportant keeps this emotion repressed by being arrogant, offensively exaggerating his or her own importance.

Defence mechanisms, like certain drugs, reduce the symptoms or manifestations of a problem without curing the ailment. Ultimately, long-term avoidance or distortion of perceived reality prevents change. Acknowledging and dealing with this reality aids effective emotional processing and problem solving.

ADDICTIONS

An addiction can be defined as any process that is compulsively utilized to avoid or distract from an unbearable reality. Those with low self-esteem can often suffer from depression. Addictive habits can be mood altering and thus, on the surface, individuals may take on board the lie that they are life enhancing. The truth of course is that some addictions can be life threatening. There follows some everyday addictions and obsessions:

- overeating
- undereating
- smoking
- alcohol and other drugs
- work
- cleaning
- gambling
- shopping
- sex
- intellectualizing feelings
- blaming others
- caretaking and helping
- religious rituals.

When caught up in an addiction or obsession, feelings do not have to be dealt with. The way forward for addicts is to start working on feeling better about themselves and learning how to cope directly with life.

AWARENESS OF FEELINGS, NEEDS AND WANTS

Low self-esteem seems to go hand in hand with a poorly defined self-concept. Low self-esteem individuals can have a vague sense of self due to their avoidance of exploring and learning more about themselves. The position seems to be that if you have an uncertain sense of self you will ultimately tend to act in a manner which precludes learning more about yourself. I can remember one client who always replied 'I don't know' any time I asked her how she was feeling. She was so 'cut off' from herself that she genuinely had no clue as to how she was feeling. If she was talking about something traumatic she would often inappropriately smile and laugh as she spoke. Similarly, another client arrived at my office on our first meeting feeling very 'confused'. She did not know how she was feeling from one minute to the next because her tendency was to feel *other people's* feelings rather than her own. Even her thoughts seemed to be those of her mother rather than originating from within herself. She had no idea of what *she* wanted or needed in her life. She had no personal identity.

If as a child your emotional needs were not met, the defensive and self-protecting behaviour that followed can make it difficult to know who you really are. Because you experience yourself as flawed in some way it can be easier to engage in the ultimate self-deceit and create a false self to live with. So, for example, if you got praise only when you were 'nice', you may take on a false self that is 'nice'. You can then hide behind this defensive facade of being friendly and always saying the 'right' thing and behaving the 'right' way. You are doing this not for the benefit of others, but so that others will think well of you and give you the positive attention you crave.

Being 'nice' all the time not only affects our ability to be a spontaneous, creative and relaxed person, but is also hard work, unreal and ultimately dishonest. It blocks the potential emotional growth of those around us because in typically 'letting them off the hook' we are depriving them of the opportunity to learn from their mistakes or inappropriate behaviour. Ultimately, being 'nice' all the time also stunts our own growth, since if we are seen as 'too nice' it may be more difficult for others to give what they perceive as honest negative feedback. Finally, because being constantly 'nice' involves hiding who you really are, how can you ever feel truly loved by anyone when you know that other people are only ever seeing what you choose for them to see?

CONTROL ISSUES

In the last section the notions of low self-esteem and the creation of a false self were linked. People who adopt a false self are very prone to feeling the need to be in control at all times. It's as if they believe that if they let their guard down they will be found out – they might expose their true self which they believe to be inadequate in some way. A need to be in control can manifest itself in a drive for power. When someone is in a powerful position they can feel less vulnerable to being 'exposed'. For instance, someone may decide to hide behind qualifications and an impressive career. Their job role can become their identity. Many such individuals often become 'workaholics'. While they are working they feel powerful.

People who have a need to be in control can also demonstrate a desire to keep life as predictable as possible. Such individuals typically avoid risk taking and are resistant to change. Rigid ways of thinking about the way things 'should be' can result in inappropriate maladaptive beliefs. The final sections of this chapter highlight how a need to control can also contribute to difficulties with decision making and have adverse effects on willingness to communicate tendencies.

DECISION MAKING

Making decisions can be difficult for those with low self-esteem since, as previously noted, such individuals having a poor sense of self are often unsure of what they want in life. In addition, the need to be perfect and the need to control the outcome of events can keep someone with low self-esteem from making a decision. The fear of taking the 'wrong' path can deter movement forward.

Frequently, a decision may appear to have been made but in reality a safe, familiar route has been chosen as a means of putting off any 'real' decision making. While pro-crastinating or playing it safe in life rather than making things happen, people are likely to end up feeling victimized by their circumstances. This, in turn, serves to erode self-esteem even further.

Melissa was dating a married man. She never knew from one day to the next when he would ring or wish to meet her. He had promised to leave his wife when the time was right – that was five years ago. Something would always happen to make him postpone such action. Melissa forever complained to her friends about the unsatisfactory nature of her situation. She felt miserable but could never come to a decision about finishing things because she said she feared the thought of being on her own. Instead, she opted for what felt familiar and safe – she continued to live in hope that her boyfriend would leave his wife sooner rather than later.

INITIATING COMMUNICATION WITH OTHERS

It was noted in Chapter 1 how our view of ourselves appears to be formed and developed from the outside inwards, arising in particular out of the experience of interacting with others. It would seem that one way to start learning about yourself is to meet with a variety of people and experiences. People with high self-esteem perceive that they can be effective in relating to others. By satisfying their needs through interaction, they view such experiences as positive. On the other hand, those with low self-esteem anticipate that relating to others will be difficult and frustrating for them. They do not expect to have their needs met in their relationships.

Research shows a relationship between low self-esteem and anxiety about communication. In relation to people who have healthy self-esteem, those with low self-esteem have been found to consider themselves less assertive, more inhibited and awkward in conversations. They feel more nervous and anxious, with expectations of failure in social settings. Such individuals also expect more negative evaluations from others than do individuals with high self-esteem.

It seems reasonable, therefore, that if you suffer from low self-esteem, in a bid to protect yourself from being in the arena of attention which for you carries with it an unpredictable outcome, you will be less willing to initiate communication than someone with a more positive view of themselves. Research in the area shows this to be the case (see p110). In extreme cases, what is known as a social phobia can develop. The most common feature of this phobia is the fear of embarrassing oneself or becoming visibly anxious while under the observation of other people.

You can explore your own 'willingness to communicate' tendencies in the scale presented in figure 2.[3] As can be seen at the end of this scale, your total score is obtained by adding up your scores for all the situations and then dividing this by 12. The highest possible 'willingness to

HOW WILLING TO COMMUNICATE ARE YOU?

Below are 12 situations in which a person might choose to communicate or not to communicate. Presume you have completely free choice. Decide the percentage of time you would choose to communicate in each type of situation. 0 = never, 100 = always.

1 Present a talk to a group of strangers.
2 Talk with an acquaintance while standing in line.
3 Talk in a large meeting of friends.
4 Talk in a small group of strangers.
5 Talk with a friend while standing in line.
6 Talk in a large meeting of acquaintances.
7 Talk with a stranger while standing in line.
8 Present a talk to a group of friends.
9 Talk in a small group of acquaintances.
10 Talk in a large meeting of strangers.
11 Talk in a small group of friends.
12 Present a talk to a group of acquaintances.

TOTAL SCORE: Add up percentages for the situations and divide by 12.

Figure 2 *'Willingness to communicate' scale*

communicate' score is 100. For our purposes here it can be taken that a score above 50 indicates a tendency towards being more willing to initiate communication with others; and below that an inclination towards being less willing to initiate communication. The higher your score the more willing you are to communicate, the lower your score the less willing you are to communicate.

This chapter has compounded the notion that there are different layers to the self. Figure 3 presents these different layers of self as discussed. The outside layer is the false self

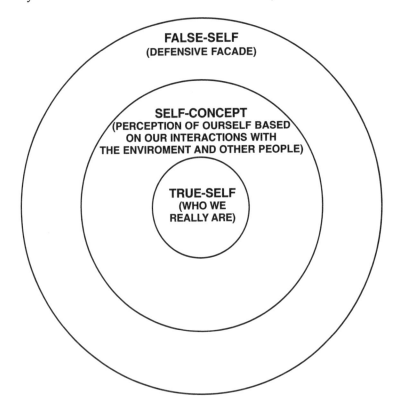

Figure 3 *The different layers of self*

(the defensive facade). If we remain living in this layer we will always feel alienated because we are forever hiding from who we truly are. If we peel back the layer of the false self, the self-concept (our perception of ourselves based on our interactions with the environment and other people, mainly in our early years) is revealed. One way to learn more about our self-concept is to meet with as many people and situations as possible to allow for an increase in positivity, realism and clarity. However, it will have become clearer throughout this chapter how the self-esteem of those around us very much colours the feedback they give us about ourselves. Therefore, what other people seem to think of us is a highly unreliable source of information upon which to base our sense of who we really are. One of the most important ways to find out about who we are and increase the positivity of our self-esteem is to have the courage to explore and tap into a deeper layer within – to come to rely more on ourselves rather than on other people for our sense of self. In the next chapter we begin this rewarding journey, which can bring with it endless possibilities.

Wherever you are in terms of your self-esteem you can learn many ways to help improve your situation. The following chapters aim to equip you with new skills and coping strategies to help you instigate positive change and move forward with your life.

CHAPTER 3

Are You Ready to Change?

'Would you tell me, please, which way I ought to go from here?'
'That depends a good deal on where you want to get to,' said the
cat. 'I don't much care where . . .' said Alice. 'Then it doesn't
matter which way you go,' said the cat.

LEWIS CARROLL[1]

Many factors can influence your readiness to start thinking and feeling better about yourself. This chapter addresses some basic issues on the topic of change in this respect. It aims to place you in the very best position to benefit from the many skills and techniques outlined in subsequent chapters. Read on and set the scene for success.

ARE YOU A 'VICTIM'?

Many of us lead our lives in 'Victim mode'. Particularly when we are suffering from low self-esteem we are prone to handing over the responsibility for ourselves to someone else. We are then not accountable when our life is not as we would wish it to be – we have other people we can blame!

Jenny was feeling very angry and low in herself when she turned up to have some counselling. She blamed the critical attitude of her parents, her controlling husband and a myriad of other people and events for the horrible feelings she was experiencing. If people and life could be better then she could be happy. Peter came to counselling with the belief that someone would have all the answers to his problems and could therefore resolve his situation for him. He presented in the first session giving minimal information, keeping his arms folded throughout. Having put no effort into the hour he spent with the counsellor, Peter came out of the session with the belief that 'counselling does not work'. Many people are like Jenny and Peter. They postpone feeling good while they sit back and wait around for someone else to make the move to sort things out. In the meantime life is passing them by. Are you a victim? The following story outlines two different ways of responding to a situation. I wonder which one you will identify with?

It was ten minutes past midnight when the fire alarm first went off. Most of the guests had already retired to their rooms for the night in this luxurious five-star hotel, chosen by many for its peaceful location in the English countryside. Once everyone had assembled outside, the fire service approached guests and informed them it was safe to go back into the hotel – it had been a false alarm. An hour later the fire alarm went off again. In fact, the guests were subjected to this on-off sequence *seven* times throughout the night!

The next morning the foyer of the hotel was full of bleary-eyed angry-looking guests. Frank queued up to speak to the receptionist. Once he had her attention he expected at a minimum some explanation for the happenings the night before. Instead, she merely smiled, pleasantly asking, 'Now, how do you wish to pay, sir?' Exasperated and not knowing quite what to say Frank went through the motions of paying, cursing under his breath as he did so.

When it came to Joe's turn to pay he immediately asked to see the duty manager of the hotel. When the duty manager appeared, Joe politely but firmly explained that he felt let down by the hotel. He reported that he would have expected from any hotel, and in particular a hotel of that calibre, an explanation of what was happening and an apology and compensation for a very disrupted night's stay. With this, the duty manager explained that the fire alarm had developed a fault which took all night to detect. He apologized for the inconvenience and asked Joe if a free weekend stay at the hotel – to be taken whenever he desired – in addition to no charge for the previous night, would constitute a satisfactory means of compensation. Joe accepted and thanked the duty manager.

Frank left the hotel feeling angry and frustrated. He was in a bad mood for the rest of the day, snapping at any little thing that did not go his way. On the other hand, Joe felt exuberant. He had taken control of the situation and obtained a result. He was pleased with his compensation, but most of all felt good about having taken some action.

Had you been one of the guests in the hotel that night, would you have opted out like Frank or taken charge like Joe? The following exercise can help you explore your 'victim status' even further.

Exercise
Are you a victim? You can get some sense of whether you are choosing the role of 'victim' in life by answering the following hypothetical questions. Compare the number of 'yes' and 'no' answers and draw your own conclusions.

1 A friend frequently asks you to look after her children while she goes shopping. You are getting annoyed with the situation. Do you have problems saying 'no' the next time she asks?

2 You and your partner/spouse have planned to go out one evening. You are feeling tired and would really prefer to have a 'cosy night in'. Do you feel unable to express your feelings?

3 You are in a new relationship. Do you find yourself apologizing for yourself or your behaviour?

4 When with friends do you nearly always end up doing what they want to do and going where they want to go?

5 Your meal in a restaurant appears to be slightly under-cooked. Do you let it pass without mentioning anything to the staff?

6 A person belonging to a cause you are not really interested in contributing to has just pushed a charity box under your nose. Rather than saying 'no thank you', do you put something in the box?

7 Do you ever find yourself complaining to friends about how others have done wrong by you?

8 On inspecting a new jacket when you have brought it home you find a small hole in one of its sleeves. Do you feel anxious at the thought of taking it back to the shop to request another?

9 A friend has turned up late *again* to go on an outing with you. Do you find it difficult to tell them how this makes you feel?

10 You hate your job. Do you feel that this is something you just have to accept?

11 You feel you may have been overcharged for your groceries. Do you avoid questioning the cashier?

12 A friend calls around to your house and is overstaying their welcome. Do you hope they will leave soon but not say anything?

13 A relative borrows some money, saying they will repay you within the week. The week has passed and they have not mentioned it. Do you feel too embarrassed to broach the topic?

14 Your relationship is going through a rough patch. Do you find you tend to blame your partner/spouse?

NO ONE CAN CHANGE YOU – BUT YOU

At the end of the day, whether you use this book on its own or in conjunction with visits to a counsellor or psycho-therapist, change will only happen when you decide to make it happen. No one can wave a magic wand and give you instant high self-esteem – change can only be instigated from within yourself. We are all independent human beings and responsible for ourselves. Only *you* can be your knight in shining armour. We are not in a position to change other people or certain events (although, interestingly, if *we* change this can sometimes have a 'knock-on effect' in certain instances). We are, however, truly in control of how we choose to react to other people and events. As adults we are also more in charge of what we decide to integrate into our self-concept. Stop blaming everything and everyone around you for how you feel. Take control and decide to put some effort into making your life the very best it can be. The past is over and done with, the future is there for you to create. Choose to start making a difference in your life *now*!

This book offers you a range of different ways to work on yourself to help you to achieve positive change. It is important to realize that reading the book will not be enough in itself. Many of the techniques will require regular and consistent practice. What are you willing to do for what you want? Your commitment will very much depend on how much you want to achieve and then maintain a more positive view of yourself.

THE WAY YOU WANT TO BE AND HOW TO GET THERE

Rather than dealing with vague notions of the way you would like things to be in your life, it is helpful to be really clear on what you desire for yourself. It makes sense to regularly ask yourself, 'What do I really want?' However, it may be difficult to know what you want if you are not in the habit of acknowledging your feelings. For example, if you have spent most of your life giving away your power to others this may have generated within you a build-up of negative emotions. Many of us do not feel that it is acceptable to process or handle such feelings externally and so very often they are suppressed. The more negative emotions are denied, the more they build up inside. To deny your feelings is to deny yourself. Only by acknowledging your true emotions can you begin to work with reality in a constructive manner, reclaiming your power and taking positive action towards clear goals. It can be useful in this respect to stop whatever you are doing a number of times a day and acknowledge to yourself in your mind how you are feeling at that moment, beginning your sentence to yourself with the words, 'I feel . . .'

Over time, as you become more self-aware and can 'tune into' your desires and feelings, setting clear goals will be so much easier. Imagine life the 'new way' by, for instance, taking specific situations, seeing in your mind the manner in which you would like to feel and act and the qualities you would wish to possess. How would that differ from the way you are now? Some people find it useful to identify a role model who exemplifies the desired behaviour, either someone they know or a person created in their minds, to help them with this work.

It goes without saying that before you can work to enhance your self-esteem, you need to want that change. However, wanting to change is not always enough in itself. Many people while wanting to change are not sure how to go about it. They keep repeating the same ways they have tried to change in the past, perhaps without clear direction, and then get frustrated when nothing alters in their life. If you feel you are not progressing in life the way you would like to, then it might be time to do something different. This book will give you plenty of scope for experimenting with different ways of working on yourself. If you feel a particular technique is not for you, simply test another one. Find what works best for you as an individual.

Exercise
1 Identify things you want to do in your life. Make your goals specific. Write down these goals (for many people committing themselves on paper makes the work more compelling!).

2 Where possible, break down main goals (short-term and long-term) into more digestible ordered steps. These in turn may be broken down into further steps. Ensure you are realistic with these goals as well as your expectation regarding the rate at which you will benefit from working on yourself.

3 Set times to review your goals and progress over the coming weeks and months to help keep you focused, but allow things to be flexible.

Remember, you are not in a race! Improvement tends to be a gradual process, and may be interspersed with times when little benefit is noticed. Plateaus or setbacks, which are generally only temporary in nature, are a normal and necessary part of the overall process of change. Be patient. Once you continue to work on yourself and your dreams, it will not be long before you are moving forward in a positive fashion once more. Be sure to take note of your intermediate successes on your journey towards your main goal. Setting and working on achieving goals is very empowering and greatly enhances self-esteem.

WHAT HAS STOPPED YOU FROM CHANGING SO FAR?

Sometimes people have an idea of how they might achieve their goals but are between two minds about change – part of them is in favour of it, another part of them feels in some way uncomfortable about it. I remember a client who came to see me after having been treated for depression and anxiety for many years. When we were exploring the way she wanted to be and why she had not made much progress towards that goal, she admitted to feeling really miserable as she was but that at least it was a 'predictable misery'. Part of her was afraid that if she started to feel better about herself, other people would pick up on this new-found confidence and perhaps as a result have higher expectations of her. She was terrified that she would let herself and others down. She felt torn in two directions – one part of her wanted to move out of the misery of the past years, while another part of her, although unhappy, felt in some way secure where she was and held her back out of fear and distrust of what increased self-esteem might bring into her life. It was a case of 'better the devil you know than the devil you don't'!

It may be that wherever you are with your level of self-esteem, you have not changed up until now because your mind, rightly or wrongly, believes that certain benefits depend on you remaining as you are – for example, the simple benefit of only having to deal with what you are familiar with. Acknowledging any pay-offs in this respect can help you become 'unstuck'. You may find an alternative, more appropriate, way of obtaining these benefits, or purely overwhelm them with the longer list of benefits available to you if you are prepared to change. The exercise that follows includes an opportunity to really sell positive change to your mind through an exploration of the benefits to be gleaned from improving your self-esteem.

Exercise
Write down any possible advantages (benefits) and disadvantages of remaining at your present level of self-esteem. Then list the advantages and any disadvantages of improving your self-esteem. Compare and contrast your lists to increase your motivation to work towards positive change.

A FEW WORDS ON THE FEELING OF FEAR

People with low self-esteem are noted for being cautious and tentative in their approach to life. Their main fear is taking risks which, as far as they are concerned, could potentially result in further loss of self-esteem. So a lot of the time they choose to 'play safe'. Things snowball as they attempt to protect their self-esteem from what they perceive as the probability of failure. Their world becomes more and more limited as they take fewer and fewer risks.

If you are waiting for fear to disappear before you change then you might be waiting for a very long time! The more you avoid fearful situations or behaviour, the more your anxiety will develop. The only way out of fear is to work through it. This can be challenging as you push out the boundaries of your 'comfort zone'; however, it definitely beats feeling helpless and living in the shadow of fear. The more you confront fear the better you will feel about yourself. Make a habit every day of tackling something small that requires you to build up courage beforehand. It may be that you have been avoiding making a certain phone call or being assertive with someone close to you. Everyone feels fear when embarking on something new – it is completely natural. You are not alone in this. As stated by Susan Jeffers: 'Feel the fear and do it anyway!'[2]

DRAW SUPPORT FROM THOSE AROUND YOU

Friendships with positive people teach you how to be positive; from those with negative people you learn how to be negative. You will benefit from having around you people who want to help and support you in your efforts to change. Be wary of those who attempt to sabotage your achievements. It may be that they have something to lose if you change from the 'old you' and suddenly start to express your own needs and wants. For example, they might not want to see the person who always used to listen to their complaining and go along with what they wanted, start disappearing before their eyes! It may be that you will have to give some thought to this area and change some of your friends. However, before doing anything rash remember that just as you will need time to become accustomed to the changes in yourself, so too will those around you need some time to adapt. The ideal situation for you would be for one of your trusted friends to decide that they too would like to improve their self-esteem! You could then work together through the skills and techniques offered by this book and encourage and motivate each other along the journey of change.

CONGRATULATE AND REWARD YOURSELF

Recently I have started going to exercise classes and I attempt to go at least twice a week. On the last day of one particular week when I had only been to the class once, I was tempted to opt out because I was feeling tired. I had the excuse that my husband had the car and so I had no means of travelling to the sports centre. However, I decided to make the effort. I ordered a taxi and arrived in good time for the class, only to find it had been cancelled! Rather than being 'fed up' because I had not achieved my goal for that week, I decided instead to acknowledge that at least I had made the effort to get to the class. No matter what the result, no matter where you are with your progress, be sure to congratulate yourself for continuing in your efforts to change.

As well as congratulating yourself on the efforts you are putting into working towards and achieving your goals, why not give yourself a special treat? This is something which so many people do not think of doing for themselves even though they may readily do so for others. Why not treat yourself today to something you would really enjoy, such as a walk, a relaxing bubble bath or a bunch of flowers? Make yourself feel the special person that you are.

Exercise
When I ask clients how they might reward themselves for making progress and taking the time to continue working on

themselves they so often look back at me blankly! Take some time to list ten ways in which you can treat yourself as a reward for your efforts to change and the achievement of your goals.

IT IS OKAY TO LOVE YOURSELF!

Certainly when I was growing up one of the worst insults someone could cast your way was, 'You love yourself!' People around me seemed to view those who loved themselves as 'big headed' or 'selfish'. This was coupled with a religion which appeared to me to relish emphasizing how we were all 'sinners' and 'unworthy'!

Loving yourself is not the same as being 'big headed'. In fact we know the opposite to be true. Low rather than high self-esteem accounts for people acting in such a way. As for being 'selfish' if you love yourself, it was noted in the previous chapter that the way we treat those around us is dependent on how we feel inside. If we feel negative about ourselves we will ultimately inflict negativity onto others, whereas if we love ourselves we are in a better position to love others. We will not be so needy and therefore will be more available to those around us. So it is not only okay to love yourself, it is actually vital if you wish to love other people more fully. Self-love begins with self-acceptance. Accept your limitations as well as your strengths. No one is perfect.

This chapter has highlighted and explored many factors that can influence your readiness to change. This basic groundwork will set you on a more solid footing for the journey that lies ahead.

CHAPTER 4

Compliments and Criticism

You should always be aware that your head creates your world.

KEN KEYES[1]

People with low self-esteem often find themselves in the unfortunate position where, because they disapprove so much of themselves, they find it difficult to accept compliments and are very sensitive to criticism from others. Despite the full information from everyday experiences indicating that they are not inadequate, their negative beliefs continue to be reinforced. With only negative information entering their already vulnerable concept of who they are, such individuals consequently continue to spiral downwards into lower self-esteem.

Before you can accept compliments and learn to handle criticism effectively it is first of all necessary to know yourself and what *you* consider your strengths and weaknesses to be. It is also important to take control of the often runaway 'inner critic' in your mind. If you feel stuck in a spiral of low self-esteem this chapter is geared towards getting you 'unstuck' and mobile in the direction of positive change. It includes work which aims to help you explore a more positive, balanced, realistic and honest view of yourself.

GETTING TO KNOW YOURSELF

Often we overvalue the opinions of others. Rather than constantly relying on the results of an assessment by other people, it is appropriate to have our own solid standards and measurements against which to gauge ourselves in all areas of our lives. The exercise that follows can be the starting point of such self-exploratory work. Once we engage in this process of learning more about ourselves we will tend not to accept, and therefore not be hurt by, every criticism that comes our way. (If we took on board absolutely every criticism thrown at us we would end up feeling very powerless indeed.) The messages incorporated in valid criticisms will get through more effectively, helping us to be more open to changes that will be to our benefit.

Exercise
1　List five of your weaknesses. (Ensure they are not complete put-downs. Imagine how your best friend who loves you would phrase them and write them down for yourself in this gentler fashion.)
2　List five of your strengths. (Again, as in part 1 of this exercise, you may like to imagine, purely as a prompt, what a best friend might write in such a list. Write down only what you can genuinely accept to be true of yourself.)

It always interests me when I ask clients to undertake this exercise, how for the most part they find it very easy to list their weaknesses (usually showing themselves no mercy!), but so often come to an abrupt halt when it comes to listing their strengths. This is akin to a sportsman placing certificates saying he 'participated but did not win' on his mantelpiece instead of displaying his trophies! Would any sportsman sell himself short like that?! If you found you had to resort to the 'best friend strategy' to help you list your strengths it may be that your mind, like that of so many people I see, works more to your disadvantage than to your advantage. You will find the next section which deals with the topic of the 'inner critic' particularly interesting. Transcribe your strengths onto a postcard to keep in your bag or diary and read them regularly. Continue to add to the list. No matter how trivial the strength seems to be, include it. (Maybe you make great chocolate cake?) Continue to work at reinforcing and progressing these strengths that bit further. For instance, if on your list you have included 'I make an effort to be pleasant with people' you might decide to enhance this strength by giving more compliments to others when they genuinely are due. Use your strengths to the full.

DEALING WITH YOUR 'INNER CRITIC' AND NEGATIVE THINKING

Your thoughts, feelings and beliefs about yourself are all interdependent (*see* figure 4). The manner in which you speak to yourself in your mind can make a dramatic difference to your self-esteem. Once you realize that your thoughts can create and reinforce your feelings about yourself it becomes clear that you are in charge of the effect

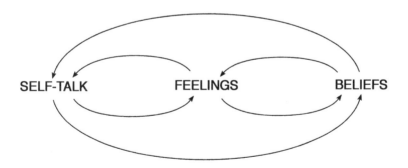

Figure 4 *The relationship between self-talk, feelings and beliefs*

life around you will have on how you value yourself. Until you interpret things in your thoughts and give them meaning you cannot experience an emotional reaction. Therefore you are in charge of influencing how you are going to feel about yourself at any particular time by choosing how you are going to allow yourself to think and interpret your world. It sounds simple but it gets results – when you change the way you think, you can ultimately change your beliefs about yourself over time.

If for the most part your self-talk is negative and critical, you will start to feel increasingly worthless. I remember one client who came to see me because despite living a very privileged life she felt useless and miserable. An examination of how she was allowing herself to speak to herself in her mind immediately shone some light on the situation. I was able to assure this client that if I were to let my thoughts 'run riot' like she did I would be feeling the very same emotions! It is interesting how many people will allow their 'inner critic' to speak to them in their minds in a manner in which they would never dream of speaking to others and would certainly find completely unacceptable coming from someone else. Individuals who treat themselves this way in their thoughts are particularly susceptible to taking critical comments from others more seriously than is often reasonable. So part of the journey towards being comfortable accepting compliments and dealing effectively with criticism from others involves learning how to combat inner criticism and negative self-talk and becoming gentler and more honest with ourselves.

You might be wondering in what ways we can be harsh and dishonest in our self-talk, adding to the negativity of an already fragile self-concept. Dr David Burns, in his *The Feeling Good Handbook*,[2] outlines some generally accepted ways we can distort our thoughts in this respect. The following are all examples of such cognitive distortions:

- *All-or-nothing thinking.* You see things in black and white. For example, if you fail a music exam you see yourself as a *complete* failure. You may go a step further and attach a negative label to yourself: 'I'm stupid.'

- *Over generalization.* You generalize from one negative experience to all other similar experiences. For instance, 'I looked after my friend's children once and it was a complete disaster. I am sure I would make a hopeless mother.'
- *Mental filter.* You pick out the negative and dwell on it to the exclusion of the positive. Every situation has a positive as well as a negative side. If you report only the negative, you are lying to yourself by omission. For example, say you attend a job interview where you are asked many questions about yourself. You answer all these questions well, but flounder slightly on one of them. You find all you can think about after the interview is *that* answer.
- *Jumping to conclusions.* This involves making a negative interpretation even though there are no definite facts that convincingly support your conclusion. For instance, a friend looks the other way as she passes you in the street and so you presume she is ignoring you. Actually, something suitable for her husband's birthday present caught her eye in a shop window and she genuinely did not see you!

This method of distorting reality can also involve always presuming that things will turn out badly in life. Interestingly enough, this can often become a self-fulfilling prophecy. By thinking in this negative way you may actually be helping what you fear most to occur! For example, taking once more the example of attending an interview, you are encouraging a negative result if you allow yourself to think beforehand, 'When I open my mouth to answer the questions I know I'll stutter.' You would be helping yourself to set things up in a more positive way by thinking in advance, 'When I open my mouth to answer the questions I can speak clearly, calmly and with confidence.'

Once you have established that you are overly negative and critical in your mind, what can you do about it? Since you own your thoughts you can control them. It makes sense to be your own best friend rather than your own worst enemy in your mind. Think of the manner in which you usually talk to yourself in your mind. Ask yourself: 'If I had a friend in my circumstances would I ever speak to them in this negative way? What tempo and tone of voice would I use? What would I say to comfort, reassure and support them while still remaining realistic?' Now decide to start speaking to yourself in the same respectful and helpful way. As in the previous chapter, praise and motivate yourself in your efforts to make a change.

If you have fallen into the habit of thinking in a critical, negative and unrealistic manner, how can you change this? I usually give clients the following task, which works in two ways: firstly, it helps to break the habit of negative thinking, and secondly, as the technique is repeatedly practised, it encourages the new habit of positive thinking. Anything you repeat often enough can become automatic.

Exercise
Starting today, become aware of how you are allowing yourself to think, and whenever you entertain a critical or negative thought, think 'stop' or see a 'stop' road sign in your mind. Then, dealing directly with the subject matter, change the negative focus of your thoughts into a positive one. Make the very best of reality as it is. Figure 5 presents a ready-made example to start you off. If the habit of negative thinking is deeply engrained, you will need to do this exercise persistently over time in your mind.

Sometimes the simple things work best in life. The impact of a critical thought containing 'I should' or 'I ought' can often be completely defused by replacing these words with 'I could'. Additionally, making changes to the nature and the

SCENARIO	CRITICAL THOUGHT	INTERRUPT	POSITIVE FOCUS
Checking through some written work you come across a mistake.	'How could I have made that mistake? I am so stupid. I never get things right.'	'Stop!'	'As usual I have been conscientious in my work. Look at how much of it I did well, and double checking it enabled me to ensure it is the very best it can be.'

Figure 5 *Challenging negative thinking*

location of an inner critical voice in your imagination can also have a positive effect. Would such a thought be less threatening, for example, if it was expressed more softly and came out of your little finger?!

YOUR SUBCONSCIOUS MIND AND THE JOURNEY OF CHANGE

To begin with, as you embark on thinking more positively, you may find yourself putting into your mind thoughts you do not fully believe. This should not surprise you since your subconscious mind will be functioning according to past conditioning.

The subconscious mind is that part of your mind of which you are unaware. It includes programmes for your entire range of feelings, beliefs and self-image. Every conscious thought is said to contribute to the building of the subconscious mind – what you put in is what you get out. So, if in the past you have been fuelling your subconscious with critical, unhelpful thoughts, negativity will probably dominate your subconscious mind at first. When your subconscious mind is fed with constructive and positive thoughts, like a creative child, it is versatile enough to explore and elaborate on these positive guidelines. Once you have heard these new, more positive, thoughts often enough to create a strong reserve at that deeper level of your mind, a more positive outlook can predominate.

This process does not have to take years. As long as they are committed to the work, clients usually report improvement after a number of weeks. Persistence with positive thoughts is the key. Repetition is important. The more positive thoughts you put into your mind the better. Every chance you get, set up every area of your life in a positive manner.

You may find it helpful initially to include on your postcard containing your strengths mentioned earlier, some positive phrases and affirmations, until your mind becomes more spontaneous in its creation of appropriate positive thoughts. There follows a list of affirmations for you to choose from to start you off:

- I am deserving.
- I am worthwhile.
- I am always going to be there for myself: I can rely on me.
- I care about myself.
- I accept myself completely.
- I allow myself to feel happy *now*.
- I give myself permission to express my feelings.
- I am powerful and creative.
- I have a lot to offer.
- I am an interesting person.
- I am loving, lovable and loved.
- I am calm, confident and in control.
- My mind is clear and focused.
- I allow myself to feel enthusiastic about life.

- With each day that passes I am becoming increasingly positive.
- I am healthy and energetic.
- I free myself from the past and I am creating a positive future.
- I am becoming a more relaxed person.
- I allow myself inner peace and serenity.
- I am ready to accept fulfillment in my life.
- I am stronger than I know.
- I choose to be in the company of positive people.
- I look forward to new experiences and challenges.
- I am nurturing appropriate positive beliefs in my mind.
- I forgive everyone in my life, including myself.
- I am making my world beautiful.

RECEIVING AND GIVING COMPLIMENTS

How do you react when someone compliments you? Many people find that they do some of the following:

- giggle/blush with embarrassment
- avoid eye contact and dismiss the compliment – for example, 'This old thing? I've had it for years and when I bought it I only paid half the price as it was in a sale!'
- cut the compliment short, often with
  a) a personal 'put down' – for instance, 'It was just pure luck that I passed the exam. I have a terrible memory.'
  or
  b) a rushed return compliment such as, 'Well, you look really good too!' (To the receiver, this usually sounds more like a means to cope with discomfort rather than a compliment from the heart.)

I was once working with a client with very low self-esteem who had an extreme reaction to compliments from others.

She reported that she 'hated herself' and thought that she was particularly ugly. Whenever anyone complimented her she would actually experience the emotion of anger. She had the harsh belief that the person giving the compliment was either 'stupid' or making fun of her.

Learning to say 'thank you' to compliments

If you were to give someone a compliment and they reacted in one of the ways listed above, just think how it would make you feel. You'd probably wish you hadn't bothered! Do yourself and the person giving you a compliment a favour – acknowledge and accept the compliment. Listen to the compliment in full, maintaining eye contact all of the time. Then smile and say 'thank you'. Return a compliment only if you are sincere about it. Wait a few moments before you do so to ensure that it can be received as a genuine compliment rather than the 'backlash' from the compliment paid to you.

Exercise
Write down a number of compliments you have received in the past, your response at that time (old response) and your preferred response (new response). Figure 6 presents a ready-made example to start you off.

Praising others

When was the last time you complimented someone? It is particularly easy to get into the habit of taking for granted those close to us, readily criticizing them and not taking the time to compliment them. Think of those around you and what you sincerely admire about them – then decide over

COMPLIMENT	OLD RESPONSE	NEW RESPONSE
'You did that piece of work really well.'	'Oh, it was nothing.'	'Thank you. It is nice to feel appreciated.'

Figure 6 *Exploring a typical and a preferred resonse to a compliment*

the next few weeks to tell them! As well as those receiving your genuine compliments, you too will benefit from this exercise. You will be training your mind to seek out positivity rather than negativity and, interestingly, the more compliments you give out the more you are inclined to get back! It is contagious!

HANDLING CRITICISM

Many people on hearing the word 'criticism' presume that it refers to something negative. However, the reality is that if you handle the challenge of criticism appropriately, it can provide you with an opportunity to learn more about and improve yourself.

Dealing with criticism from others

Many people have a great deal of trouble dealing with criticism. It can cause them to feel that they are being attacked and, therefore, it is no surprise that they get defensive. Research shows that individuals with low self-esteem are more prone to engage in defensive behaviour than those with high self-esteem. When someone criticizes you, rather than immediately becoming defensive, take a deep breath and step back, working through the following stages in your mind:

- Listen to the criticism in full.
- Is the criticism true or false?
- Acknowledge any truth in the criticism.

We will now examine each of these stages in more detail.

Listen to the criticism in full

Allow the person criticizing you to express fully their negative feelings and to feel that they have been heard before you 'jump in'. A client of mine reported that she felt she had to constantly criticize her husband because 'he never listens'. She desperately wanted to feel heard. One useful and delightfully simple technique in this respect is called 'mirroring'. It involves listening to what the person says and then saying it back, using, as far as possible, the *same* words (not your interpretation of these words) so the person knows you have heard *exactly* what was said. This also ensures of course that you respond to the criticism given rather than what you *think* the criticism is about. I remember myself and my husband Mark using this approach once while sitting in a coffee shop. It went something like this:

Mark: When we are having an argument you very often interrupt me before I have completed what I want to say.
Elaine: I hear you saying that when we are having an argument I very often interrupt you before you have completed what you want to say.

Despite the fact that a woman at the table beside us was listening with great interest, I continued to pursue the mirroring technique! It put me in a good position for handling Mark's criticism. He felt listened to (which in itself calmed him considerably) and I knew I had heard his criticism correctly. Repeating his words also put me in a better position to empathize with him – to get a sense of how he might be feeling.

True or false?

Once we know that we have heard the criticism correctly it is important for us to discern what type of criticism it is: is there any truth in the criticism or is the criticism really telling us more about the person giving it? Ask yourself, 'Could there be any truth in what has been said?' If you are feeling particularly uptight as a result of the statement it may actually have hit on one of your 'weaknesses'. On occasions it may be that you need more information before you can decide whether the criticism is true or false, or even if it is a bit of both! For instance, if a criticism is generalized, such as, 'You are unreasonable', you may need to ask for more specific information. Such a criticism may be true in one situation, but generally you may know it to be false.

Acknowledge the truth

If there is even a glimmer of truth in the criticism (here comes the hard bit!), *acknowledge it*. It takes courage to be honest with yourself as well as with the other person in this respect. Usually this acknowledgement has a calming effect on the person giving out the criticism. He or she will tend to start backing down a bit at this point. There is no need to over-apologize or belittle yourself when acknowledging the truth in a criticism. Examine the following example:

Boss: There are a lot of errors in this report.
Employee: You are right. I left it to the last minute to type up and consequently did not allow myself enough time to check through it in the manner I usually would. Next time I will ensure I put aside an adequate amount of time for the work. Thank you for highlighting this issue for me.

If, having been open to the criticism, you cannot see any truth in it, trust your belief in yourself and go ahead and reject the criticism without apology. Express yourself with 'I feel' statements rather than apportioning blame and getting involved in an argument. Let us look at the 'boss and employee' situation once more:

Boss: You are always careless with your work.
Employee: I do not accept that at all. On the contrary, I am usually very careful with my work. I feel hurt that you would think that.

Exercise
Think of a number of criticisms that have been levelled at you in the past. As in the example in figure 7, clearly outline the criticism. Give your response at that time (old response). Ask yourself whether there was any truth in the criticism. Be honest with yourself. Acknowledge whether or not the criticism was in some way valid. Finish off by writing out your preferred response (new response). If a criticism has been invalid be sure to counteract it fully by engaging your mind in relevant, positive, supportive self-talk. This becomes easier with practice!

OUTLINE CRITICISM	OLD RESPONSE	TRUE OR FALSE?	NEW RESPONSE
'I don't think you love me. You are always locked away in your room studying for exams.'	'You are so selfish and self-absorbed. You think only about yourself.'	False	'That is simply not true. I do love you. I feel under pressure because my exams are so close.'

Figure 7 *Working through a criticism*

Giving useful criticism

As we have seen, criticism does not have to be a bad thing. It frequently involves giving constructive feedback. People can learn a lot about themselves from such criticism and may even wish to ask the person offering the criticism some questions so that they can clarify areas for positive change. However, you need to be aware that individuals also criticize for a number of other reasons:

- They may have opinions different from those of the person they are criticizing.
- They may be having a bad day.
- They may be jealous or wanting to take revenge.
- They may, unconsciously, be projecting their own faults on to the person they are criticizing (see Chapter 2). If this is the case it is really themselves they are criticizing, not the other person. In a similar vein, there is an old saying which states that we criticize most in others what we dislike about ourselves.

When preparing to give criticism to others, be very aware of your reason for doing so. Are you really wanting to provide honest feedback or is another motive involved?

When actually giving the criticism, it helps to keep to the point, balancing the criticism with an acknowledgement of something positive about the person: 'I appreciate how thorough you are being with this work. We do, however, need to move things along a bit quicker to meet the deadline.' Avoid labelling the person. Direct your criticism at their *behaviour* and let them know how it makes you feel. Rather than saying, 'You are a selfish person' you might say, 'I found what you did just now selfish. I feel frustrated.' Let them know you have taken the time to see things from their perspective: 'I know you have been feeling under a lot of pressure lately . . .'

When you are completing your criticism be clear and constructive in your suggestions for any changes in behaviour you are hoping for: 'In future, I would like you and our other receptionist to take your lunch breaks at different times.' Always allow time for the person you have criticized to respond to what you have said. Listening carefully to their reply is a vital part of the whole process, ensuring that you fully understand their position.

Taking time to view yourself more honestly and positively can enable you to develop a more solid sense of yourself and your worth. As you come to appreciate yourself more you will be increasingly open to receiving and giving compliments. The challenge of receiving and giving criticism can be seen as an opportunity that gives you additional scope for discovering more about yourself.

This chapter, in its treatment of handling compliments and criticism, touches on the territory of assertiveness training. The next chapter, which deals with anger management, also incorporates the notion of becoming more assertive. I once remember asking a very timid client of mine if she would like to work at expressing herself and standing up for herself more. Her initial response was to flatly refuse because in her words: 'I would prefer to be pleasant and nice to people!' Many individuals presume that being assertive involves being pushy or aggressive. However, this is not what assertiveness is about. Being assertive is being honest about who you really are, and communicating with respect what you think and feel. Rather than hoping that others will be able to mind read, an assertive person takes responsibility for their own wants and needs. Being assertive is about getting a result in a firm but polite manner. Assertiveness, like any skill, can be learnt and practised.

CHAPTER 5

Managing Your Anger

A man who is sure of himself is not angry at every slight done him, nor does he carry grudges. A man who fears for his own worth, however, is furious under such conditions.

JANE ROBERTS[1]

Within the area of managing emotions, it is those feelings which can be problematic that are of most interest. The emotion of anger tends to be a particularly strong one, experienced when we feel threatened, frustrated, hurt or 'hard done by'. Consequently, it is not surprising that so many people experience difficulties in dealing with it. This chapter makes two assumptions regarding the area of anger management: a) Anger can be either healthy or inappropriate depending on the nature of the beliefs underlying the emotion, b) It is important to have positive strategies for handling both forms of anger.

When anger is healthy it can serve as a helpful reminder that all is not the way we would like it to be and therefore can spur us on to take some action to change things for the better and further our goals. In contrast, as this chapter will highlight, inappropriate anger can be a very destructive emotion. Both forms of anger bring up the important subject of coping.

Coping can be problem-focused and/or emotion-focused. Problem-focused coping is external and involves dealing directly with the cause of anger. For example, if you experience bad service in a restaurant you can ask to speak to the manager and so voice your feelings and get a positive result. Problem-focused coping very often entails learning how to become more assertive. Emotion-focused coping involves working internally with anger in a positive manner. It becomes particularly relevant when, for example, the anger is arising from inappropriate beliefs or the circumstances you are responding to with anger are difficult to control. This form of coping can involve reappraising/re-interpreting beliefs and learning to become more relaxed.

As this chapter progresses, it will explore in some detail ways to manage your emotions. However, it is interesting initially to examine why coping with anger is particularly relevant to sufferers of low self-esteem.

ANGER AND LOW SELF-ESTEEM

Research exploring the need for consistency and predictability of the 'self' has found that people with low self-esteem tend to zone in on what they perceive as negative rather than positive feedback from others in an attempt to maintain their previously formed view of themselves. They have a craving for positive feedback in their hearts but their beliefs about themselves in their heads do not allow them to believe they deserve it. This is what Swann and his colleagues term 'affective-emotional crossfire'.[2] It is the crossfire between what individuals *want* to believe and what they *think* might be accurate feedback from others.

This mechanism of scanning for negative feedback from others can help us understand how many of the unhealthy thought distortions and inappropriate beliefs outlined in this book can come into play in our lives if we are suffering from low self-esteem. It is a means of continuously confirming for ourselves the concept of our identity. So, people with low self-esteem are more likely than those with high self-esteem to take things personally and regard other people's actions as an attack on them even when this was not intended. Emotionally, because they desire to think well of themselves and have others think well of them, they can feel deeply hurt and threatened by what they are perceiving and can ultimately become defensive and self-protecting. They are prime candidates for experiencing inappropriate anger.

I remember seeing a client who wanted help with her angry and jealous feelings which were threatening her relationship with her boyfriend. Whenever her boyfriend spoke with or even looked in the direction of another woman she inappropriately believed that this proved that she was unattractive and worthless. No matter how much he assured her that he found her attractive and loved her, she could not believe him. What he was telling her was inconsistent with her inappropriate belief. Ultimately she experienced inappropriate anger which was directed at her boyfriend even if he so much as glimpsed at another woman. She was blaming him for her own sense of inadequacy.

CAN YOU BE IN CONTROL OF YOUR FEELINGS?

Many people presume that emotions just 'happen' to them – that they have no choice in the matter whatsoever. However, a psychotherapeutic approach known as Rational Emotive Behaviour Therapy suggests that our emotions are not directly caused by what happens to us, but rather are based largely on our beliefs. Therefore, to the extent that our emotions are based on our beliefs we can have some amount of control over them. In taking on board responsibility for what we believe, we can be more open to the idea of being responsible for our emotions. Distinctions can be made between healthy or inappropriate anger depending on whether the beliefs underlying the emotion are healthy or inappropriate.

Inappropriate beliefs/inappropriate anger

In Chapters 2 and 4 we touched on the area of how we can
distort reality in our minds in ways which are ultimately to
the disadvantage of our self-esteem. It also happens that
when we have a very rigid view about the way things
'should be' in life we can end up with an inappropriate
maladaptive belief system. This can include four beliefs
suggested by Rational Emotive Behaviour Therapy and
which Dr Windy Dryden outlines in detail in his book
Overcoming Anger.[3] I use the mnemonic 'ALSO' to remember
them:

- **A**wfulizing
- **L**ow frustration tolerance
- **S**elf-damnation
- **O**ther-damnation

The nature of these beliefs will now be briefly examined.

Awfulizing beliefs

These involve over-reacting in our mind in terms of how
'awful' it is when an event does not conform to our rigid
expectation. For example, Helen has a rigid belief that her
husband should always ring her from work at 1pm each day.
One day she is by the phone waiting for him to ring -he is
already 15 minutes late. She keeps looking at her watch and
acting like it is 'the end of the world'. Helen is experiencing
inappropriate anger. The more she tells herself how awful
the situation is, the angrier she becomes. It is not good that
she is waiting around for his call but it is not *that* terrible. By
the time he does get to ring her his explanation of why he is
ringing late is drowned out by her shouts of irrational abuse.
All her husband hears is his wife 'ranting and raving'.
Awfulizing beliefs are unrealistic. The fact is, things often
happen in life to cause people to be occasionally late. Such
beliefs are also unhelpful. What did Helen manage to

achieve? She made herself feel incredibly angry and made her husband wonder why he'd bothered to ring her at all!

Low frustration tolerance beliefs

These entail believing that we cannot and should not have to endure the event which we are responding to with inappropriate anger. As Helen paces up and down looking at her watch she might be thinking, 'I can't stand this. I should not have to wait like this. I can't tolerate being frustrated.' Low frustration tolerance beliefs are unrealistic. Helen *can* endure waiting a bit longer for her husband to ring (what is the worst thing that could happen to her as a result of having to wait?). Again, as with awfulizing beliefs, low frustration tolerance beliefs are completely unhelpful for dealing with the event at hand.

Self-damnation beliefs

These involve having negative and condemning beliefs about ourselves which we perceive as being highlighted by other people. So for instance, when Helen's husband is late ringing her, she comes to the conclusion that it must be her fault. Perhaps he is ringing late because she was irritable that morning before he went off to work. Helen condemns herself if she ever becomes irritable. If she is irritable, she feels she is 'bad'. The inappropriate anger is directed at her husband for reminding her of what she condemns about herself. This in turn serves as a self-protective strategy, distracting her from herself – her husband becomes the focus of the condemnation. Self-damning beliefs are unrealistic and unhelpful. If Helen looked at the 'wider picture' she would find much evidence to support the fact that she is not a 'bad' person – for example, she is a 'good' mother. All that she has achieved is that she has become inappropriately angry and dished out abuse to her husband.

Other-damnation beliefs

These beliefs entail condemning the 'whole' of another person as a result of one offence. So, because Helen's husband rang late she may conclude that he is 'a terrible person'. Other-damnation beliefs are unrealistic and unhelpful. No one can be defined by one piece of behaviour. Helen is left feeling inappropriately angry and her husband feels she is being completely irrational – which of course she is!

Healthy beliefs/healthy anger

When we are flexible in our mind about the way things can turn out in life, an appropriate and healthy belief system can develop. This can include beliefs which are directly opposite to those listed in the last section and you will notice that they are more realistic than the inappropriate beliefs reviewed. Had Helen held these beliefs while waiting for her husband to ring, they would have helped her to experience healthy anger and to communicate with him in a more productive manner when he eventually did ring. Healthy beliefs can include: anti-awfulizing, high frustration tolerance, self-acceptance and other-acceptance. Each of these will now be briefly examined in turn.

Anti-awfulizing beliefs

These involve acknowledging that although an event may be far from satisfactory, it is not the 'end of the world'. Helen could have thought to herself when her husband was late ringing her: 'It is a nuisance that he is late ringing, but it is not disastrous.'

High frustration tolerance beliefs

These beliefs entail the appreciation that we can endure frustration. When her husband was late ringing her, Helen could have concluded: 'I am finding it frustrating waiting for his call, but I can tolerate it.'

Self-acceptance beliefs

Such beliefs involve being able to appreciate that although at times we may not behave well, such behaviour does not make us a bad person. Instead of presuming that her husband ringing late was evidence that she must have upset him by being irritable that morning, Helen could have decided to say to herself: 'I appreciate there are times when I may be irritable. This just shows I am a human being. Overall I am a good person.' (Of course, Helen is also jumping to the conclusion here that her husband ringing late is something to do with her. As it happened his work overran and he had to take a later lunch!)

Other-acceptance beliefs

These beliefs involve accepting that other people are human and therefore will sometimes not do things the way we want them to. Helen could have appreciated the following: 'My husband let me down by not ringing me when he said he would, but he is a human being and so cannot always be expected to get things right. Overall he is a good person.'

THE IMPORTANCE OF ALTERING INAPPROPRIATE BELIEFS

As noted in the previous chapter, the process of altering beliefs does not have to take years. Once you are committed to the work, improvements can be noticed in a matter of weeks. Consistently working to become more flexible and realistic in the way you choose to view life and speak to yourself in your mind can in time replace inappropriate beliefs with healthier beliefs (*see* figure 8). This in turn can help you to experience healthy rather than inappropriate anger in life.

It is particularly important to cut inappropriate anger out of our lives as much as possible, since inappropriate anger usually translates into frequent or chronic anger which can have serious consequences for our health. The physical manifestations of anger are akin to those of anxiety. They include palpitations, a rise in blood pressure, quickening of the breathing and an increase in muscle tension. The effects of anger and anxiety are designed to arouse the body to a state which provides the maximum physical energy for quick action in the face of a perceived threat or hurt. It was only ever intended to be a temporary state to be called on in 'emergencies'. Inappropriate anger can result in unneces-

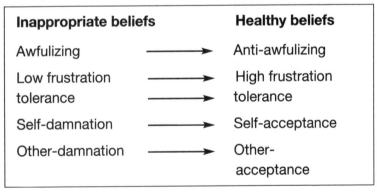

Inappropriate beliefs	Healthy beliefs
Awfulizing	Anti-awfulizing
Low frustration tolerance	High frustration tolerance
Self-damnation	Self-acceptance
Other-damnation	Other-acceptance

Figure 8 *Inappropriate and healthy beliefs*

sary strain being placed on the body. Research shows that the physical effects of chronic sustained anger can embrace hypertension, damaged and blocked arteries, raised cholesterol levels and increased susceptibility to infection. Mental associations can include depression, hostile attitudes and feelings of fear, panic and apprehension. Concentration, attention, memory and judgement can all be adversely affected. Obviously, none of this is going to enhance how you feel about yourself.

WHAT ARE YOU AFRAID OF?

As well as working to ensure our anger is healthy we also need to ensure that we handle this healthy anger to our advantage. Many people feel uncomfortable with the notion of expressing anger. Often, as children, when we are taught to be 'good' and 'nice' this does not allow for the expression of anger. Therefore, many people are left at a loss as to what they should do with such feelings. Some individuals actually feel ashamed of experiencing anger and often will work to hide it from others. They will sometimes even hide it from themselves by repressing angry feelings. The following exercise, which is adapted from the work of Gael Lindenfield,[4] may help you to gain some insight into your present means of dealing with anger. It requires you to reflect on your childhood perceptions of the management of anger by those around you.

Exercise
1 Write down your perception of how your mother (or mother substitute) handled her anger.
2 Write down your perception of how your father (or father substitute) handled his anger.
3 How did your parents react towards you if you expressed anger?
4 In light of what you have written in response to the last three questions, write out what beliefs regarding the

management of anger you feel you carry with you from childhood.

5 What does the logical and rational part of your mind make of these beliefs? Does it agree or disagree with them? Indicate those which you agree with and those which you disagree with.

Many people with whom I have worked through this exercise have expressed how uncomfortable they were with their parents' behaviour. Many of them even felt angry about it! It is important to remember that parents can only teach what they themselves have been taught. By becoming more self-aware and continuing to work on yourself you can choose what your children will learn from you.

People's fears about expressing anger often rest on the belief that they may hurt other people's feelings or end up being rejected as a result of expressing how they feel. Martha's mother would ring her every evening for a chat. She had fallen into this habit since the death of her husband five years before and she made a point of always stating how she only lived for that contact with her daughter. Martha felt angry about her mother not appreciating that after having worked all day at the office the evening was her time for catching up with household chores and spending time with her own daughter and husband. She really did not have the time for these long phone calls. However, she continued to bottle up her anger rather than take the risk of upsetting her mother.

When Martha came to see me we explored how she was being emotionally blackmailed by her mother. She felt completely controlled by her. It became important for Martha to realize that she was not responsible for her mother's misery or for helping her to overcome her loneliness. It was selfish of Martha's mother to expect her daughter to 'prop up her life'. It was her own responsibility to create a new life following the death of her husband.

Martha decided to help her mother, but on her own terms. Time with her own family had also to be taken into account.

For many of us, if someone rejects us it can make us feel worthless. So in order to receive approval from others we act in the manner in which we feel others want us to act. This may mean keeping a lid on our anger.

Margery's neighbour Janet always asked her to go into town with her whenever she was choosing something new for her house. Margery felt angry that Janet expected her to drop everything she was doing whenever she decided it was time to go on a shopping trip. However, she worried so much about what other people thought about her that she would always find herself replying, 'Of course I would love to come shopping with you!' Beneath her smile she was furious. Interestingly, Margery was so busy striving to obtain approval from those around her that she overlooked the fact that she was not earning their respect. By doing everything her neighbour wanted, Margery was increasingly being taken for granted by Janet.

EXPRESSING HEALTHY ANGER ASSERTIVELY

It is okay to express healthy anger! However, some ways of letting your feelings be known are more appropriate and acceptable than others. You may find the following guidelines useful. Note how many of them overlap with suggestions offered in the previous chapter for the related area of giving useful criticism. It is appropriate to take control when you first notice any annoyance rather than waiting for things to escalate.

- Be aware of your reason for wanting to express your feelings. What is your goal in the situation? Do you want to blame and lash out rather than give genuine feedback?

- What price might you pay for revealing how you feel and will it be worth it? For instance, if you feel your boss is not the type of person who will take kindly to you expressing your anger and you really want to keep your job you may decide to use another strategy for dealing with your anger, such as relaxation techniques (see later in this chapter).
- Prepare a plan of what you wish to say in advance. Ensure that it is clear and to the point.
- Get the attention of the person you wish to speak to – for example, 'I wish to speak to you for two minutes. Is this a good time?'
- Own your statements – instead of saying 'You make me angry . . .' say 'I feel angry when you . . .'
- Avoid labelling people. Let them know how their *behaviour* makes you feel – for instance, 'I feel angry and humiliated when you shout at me in front of our friends.'
- Wherever possible balance the expression of your anger with an acknowledgement of something positive about the person – for instance, 'I feel I can say this to you because I consider you to be one of my very best friends.'
- Listen to what the other person may wish to say on the matter.
- Be clear and specific about any requests you wish to make – such as, 'I would appreciate in future when borrowing any of my books that you come and ask me first.' If you do not feel that you have been heard, repeat your request. Look for agreement to your request.
- Match your body language to what you are saying – you will not be taken seriously if you are expressing feelings of anger and smiling at the same time!

Exercise
Think of a number of situations in your life where you felt healthy anger towards someone. As in the ready-made example in figure 9, outline what you felt angry about. Give

your response at that time (old response). Finish off by writing out your preferred response (new response).

SITUATION WHERE YOU FELT ANGRY	REASON FOR ANGER	OLD RESPONSE	NEW RESPONSE
My birthday party last year	A man said: 'All women are bad drivers.'	Remained angry in silence.	To the man: 'I feel angered by your comments about women drivers. I would appreciate if you would refrain from making such comments in my company.'

Figure 9 *Working through a past situation involving angry feelings*

FORGIVENESS

Forgiveness is very often one of the most important virtues you need in order to fully release anger. When you withhold forgiveness *you* suffer; very often the 'offender' is completely unaware of the torment you are putting yourself through! This person will continue to enjoy life while you clutter your soul with unpleasant feelings. Even worse, it may be that you are forever throwing things into the face of the 'offender' long after you have expressed your anger – all because you do not wish to forgive and let go. Shakti Gawain outlines some wonderful techniques for forgiveness and release in her inspirational book entitled *Creative Visualization.*[5] The following exercises in this section are adapted from her work.

Exercise

1 Write down on a sheet of paper all the people you can think of in your life who have ever hurt you in any way.

2 Beside each name write down what it was that the person did that prompted you to hold negative feelings towards them.

3 Close your eyes and imagine each person in turn in front of you. Explain to them that you wish to forgive them for past hurt. You may choose words such as: 'I forgive you and set you free. My heart sends you love. Be happy and at peace.'

4 As you speak to each person allow yourself to become aware of a feeling of relief and lightness inside. Some individuals also report sensing a feeling of warmth in their heart.

5 When this process has come to an end, open your eyes feeling refreshed, calm and alert. On your piece of paper write alongside each person listed, 'I forgive you and set you free.' Tear up the piece of paper and throw it away.

6 If you feel you need to, you can repeat this exercise from time to time as appropriate.

Sometimes forgiving yourself can be even harder than forgiving others. I remember a client named Steven who came to see me. He revealed how three years previously he had planned to stay with his father for Christmas. His father wanted him to come home on the 23rd of December, but Steven decided he would wait until Christmas Eve, so that he could tie up some final pieces of work at the office. At 10pm on the 23rd the phone rang. It was the hospital ringing to break the sad news that his father had been knocked down by a car and had died on his way to hospital.

Steven was completely devastated by the news. For three years he chastised himself for not going to stay with his father on the day he had suggested. His health started to deteriorate. He complained of stomach cramps and persistent headaches and reported that he was frequently catching viral infections and had lost a significant amount of weight. He revealed that he felt anxious and panicky a lot of the time and that his confidence was at an all-time low.

Before Steven could move forward with his life in a positive way it was important for him to let go of the anger he was directing towards himself everyday. Part of that process involved coming to the decision to forgive himself. I had an experience in part similar to Steven's, in that I too felt angry with myself for not being present at a parent's death. My mother was dying of cancer and it came to a point where we knew that the end was near. My brother Trevor and I had kept a vigil by her bedside for 48 hours and were feeling completely drained and exhausted. We decided to leave the hospital for a few hours' sleep, leaving my father on his own by my mother's bedside. When we returned three hours later we were told that my mother had passed away about 10 minutes earlier. I remember being so angry with myself for leaving the hospital that morning. For a period afterwards I tormented myself with 'if only'. In time I realized that for the sake of my wellbeing and peace of mind, I had to forgive myself and let go of the anger. I came to accept that I did the very best I could under the circumstances.

If you have not forgiven yourself for something in the past, I would like to suggest that you have suffered enough. How will prolonging the agony help things? You have a choice: you can wear yourself down with your angry feelings, or you can forgive yourself and get on with your life. It is up to you!

The following exercise follows along the very same lines as the 'offering of forgiveness to others' technique outlined earlier in this section. However, here you are *receiving* the forgiveness, both from yourself and others.

Exercise

1 Write down on a sheet of paper all the people you can think of in your life who you have ever hurt in any way. Allow one of these people to be yourself.

2 Beside each name write down what it was you did that prompted negative feelings.

3 Close your eyes and imagine each person in turn in front of you. When you meet with 'yourself', allow the representation before you to symbolize the most wise and loving part of you. Explain to each person how you feel you did them wrong and ask for their forgiveness.

4 Allow yourself to hear each person saying how they forgive you and wish you peace and happiness. Notice how you feel throughout this process.

5 When you have heard from everyone, open your eyes feeling refreshed, calm and alert. Write on the sheet, 'I am forgiven and I forgive myself.' Tear up the piece of paper and throw it away.

6 Affirm to yourself: 'Now I am free.'

7 If you feel you need to, you can repeat this exercise from time to time as appropriate.

LEARNING TO RELAX

Since ancient times man has been curious about the manner in which the mind and body co-exist. While many have put forward the idea that they operate separately, recent research on the subject suggests that they work in unison. Studies support the concept of 'holistic medicine', which views the human being as an integrated 'whole'. Mental and emotional experiences can be seen to produce changes in the body. For example, I have written elsewhere on the dramatic effect the mind can have on physical pain – not only on the perception of such pain but also on the level of endorphins (the body's natural painkillers) released in the body[6&7]. Earlier in this chapter, it was noted how the emotion of anger can produce definite reactions in the body. The effects outlined are the same as that produced by the feeling of anxiety, arousing the body to a state of readiness for action in the face of perceived threat. Similarly, physical processes can influence the mind. For instance, when coffee containing caffeine is consumed the central nervous system is stimulated and levels of concentration and alertness are increased. If your heart and breathing rate increase and tension is stored in your muscles this will also have an effect on how you feel mentally. It is very difficult to feel emotionally calm when the body is in such a state.

In the previous sections of this chapter the main focus was on a psychological approach to helping yourself. The current and subsequent section address the other side of the coin: the many positive ways in which you can work with the body to benefit your state of mind in the face of potential anger.

Periodically check your state of physical relaxation

To avoid a build-up of stress in the body, it makes sense to check out from time to time how your body is feeling throughout the day. In his book *The Stress Factor*,[8] Dr Stanton recommends focusing on certain key body areas: the hands, the brow, the jaw and the abdomen. If the muscles feel tense you may wish to slowly clench them a bit more and hold this tension for a moment. Then let the tension go very gradually. As far as the jaw is concerned, Dr Stanton notes how a good yawn is probably the most effective way of relieving tension!

Should you wish for even greater relaxation you can continue this tensing and relaxing, working through the other muscle groups of the body – calves, thighs, buttocks, chest, back, arms, shoulders and neck. Enjoy the sense of comfort and relaxation that follows. Be patient and practise. Gaining confidence with this technique will allow you to relax anywhere, any time you need to release tension.

Relax your breathing

When confronted with a situation which you are responding to with angry feelings, some simple breathing exercises can help you to calm down and become more in control. Accompanying such exercises with positive self-talk, such as, 'I am feeling calm, confident and in control', can have a profound effect and improve things even further. Because of their obvious relevance to anger as well as anxiety management, I have adapted the following breathing exercises from my book entitled *Anxiety, Phobias and Panic Attacks*.[9] They include many of the ideas put forward by Beata Jencks on the subject.[10] Take time to experiment to help you find out which techniques benefit you the most when you wish to become calmer.

- Place your hands over the area around your navel and focus your attention there. (According to Taoist philosophy this area is the seat of 'chi', the body's centre of energy.) Begin inhaling deeply, expanding your stomach as much as possible so that your hands rise gently. Now exhale, taking twice as long as you did to inhale, pulling your abdomen muscles in and noticing the fall of the hands. Repeat.
- Imagine a deep well in your abdomen. As you breathe imagine that you are following a dropped stone on its fall down the well during each exhalation.
- Keeping your shoulders still, imagine inhaling through the fingertips, up the arms into the shoulders and then exhaling down the trunk into the abdomen and legs and out of the toes. As you breathe in, allow comfort and calm to enter your body. Cleanse your body of any tensions with the out breath. Repeat.
- As you breathe, imagine you are inhaling a bronchodilator agent which relaxes and widens the walls of the bronchi (the tubes in the lungs), allowing the air to stream in easily. As you exhale notice the soft collapse of these air passages. Repeat.
- For two or three respiratory cycles imagine your breath is flowing with ocean waves or tides. Feel the passive flowing in and out.
- Imagine inhaling and exhaling through the skin on any

part of your body. On each inhalation allow the skin to feel refreshed and invigorated. On each exhalation permit the skin to relax.

LOOKING AFTER YOURSELF

If you want to feel good in yourself and perform at your best you need to look after yourself. This will involve the commonsense notions of ensuring that you eat well and take some exercise. Most of the time we all know what we need to do to take better care of ourselves. Usually it is just a case of making a decision to be more committed to doing it!

Eating a well-balanced diet including fresh fruit and vegetables, nuts, starches, fish, meat and poultry can help to strengthen your body's ability to withstand stress. Symptoms of anxiety (which are often linked with chronic sustained anger) can be exacerbated by certain foods. Whenever you can it is wise to limit the amount of caffeine, dairy products, alcohol and foods containing sugar. Take charge of what you are eating – it makes sense to become more aware of what you are putting into your body.

Exercising is a wonderful way to release tension. It also has the added benefit of releasing endorphins into the bloodstream, which explains the sense of wellbeing that can be experienced afterwards. Following exercise, both the body and mind feel calmer. Before embarking on an exercise programme I would recommend you speak to your doctor. Build up your exercise programme gently.

It can often be most challenging to contemplate changing an emotion when you are fully immersed in the full-blown feeling of it. If in the early stages of your work on yourself you ever feel the physiology of your body changing and that angry feeling beginning to 'come on strong', you may choose to stand back and take some time away from things. This will give you time to regain control and ensure that if you consider it appropriate to state your feelings, you can do so in a calm, rational and assertive manner.

The key to long-term change involves 'nipping things in the bud'. Taking better care of yourself can include the benefit of helping you to feel more in charge of your life. Engaging yourself in the important groundwork outlined to help combat negative thinking and inappropriate beliefs, and working towards becoming a more relaxed person in general, can help to ensure that any anger you are feeling is healthy anger. When such feelings are then appropriately handled with your new-found skills, they have the potential to fuel positive changes in your life. As well as benefiting your mental and physical health, effective anger management will greatly enhance how you feel about yourself.

CHAPTER 6

Visualizations for a More Positive Future

Any idea seriously entertained tends to bring about the realization of itself.

JOSEPH CHILTON PEARCE[1]

In Chapter 4 it was noted how working in a positive manner with your 'self-talk' can be very much to your advantage, over time helping to create a more positive view of yourself at a subconscious level. Your imagination can also be used in many ways to enhance your self-esteem. In particular the use of imagery can be a very powerful means of working on yourself, since any one image can be worth literally hundreds of words. Imagery is often claimed to be the language of the deeper part of the mind.

In this chapter a range of visualization techniques will be explored under the following headings: boosting confidence, fully appreciating yourself, handling internal conflict and freeing yourself from attachment to others. Choose those which seem most appropriate to your own circumstances for everyday use. Before embarking on this work it will first of all be useful to examine how your imagination works for you as an individual.

LEARNING ABOUT YOUR IMAGINATION

It was Aristotle who stated, 'The soul never thinks without a picture.' The fact is of course that we have four other senses in addition to sight – hearing, smell, touch and taste. People can vary in the importance they place on each of these senses when taking in information about the world and using them in their imagination. Although most people will have moments when they use all of the senses, the rest of the time they may be more attentive to only one or two of them. For example, artists are claimed to be very 'visual' while musicians are said to favour 'auditory' input.

To highlight the way you utilize your senses in your imagination, experiment with each of the following in figure 10, which initially appeared in my book on self-hypnosis.[2] If you find some easier than others then you more than likely

Visual (sight)	Auditory (hearing)	Kinesthetic (touch)
Imagine what your favourite room at home looks like. See in your mind the face of someone you love.	Hear your favourite piece of music in your mind. Imagine the sound of someone calling your name.	Imagine placing your hand under a tap of running water. Feel in your mind the sensation of shaking hands with someone.

Olfactory (smell)		Gustatory (taste)
Breathe in the smell of freshly cut flowers in your mind. Imagine the smell of your favourite meal.		Taste your favourite meal in your mind. Imagine that tangy taste when you place a segment of orange in your mouth.

Figure 10 *Testing your senses in your imagination*

have identified your predominant senses. On the other hand, you may not experience any dramatic differences between your senses at all. See how it goes! If your visual sense appears to be weak, know that it can be trained with practice. Usually leading from a predominant sense to a weaker one can help in this respect. For instance, if your sense of smell is very strong in your imagination, it may help to imagine first the smell of your favourite meal, which can then 'lead' you on to a visual image of that meal in your mind. To improve the skill of your use of any sense in your imagination, practice is the key.

BOOSTING CONFIDENCE

A technique known as mental rehearsal is particularly useful for boosting confidence and helping with the achievement of a positive outcome in specific situations. It simply involves, as the name suggests, rehearsing in your mind the way you want to be in any area of your life – visualizing yourself the very best way you can realistically be. Before I present a seminar I will persistently rehearse in my imagination the prospective scenario, seeing myself looking and feeling comfortable and at ease in front of the audience and speaking clearly, calmly and with confidence. Imagining in this way over and over again impresses a positive attitude deep within me, helping to override any past negative beliefs.

A lot of the time we get what we expect from life. If you set things up in a positive way in your mind you will attract positive outcomes and help yourself to realize your full potential. Isolate particular areas in your life where you wish to be more confident and work on each of these in turn. For instance, if you wish to improve your confidence in social settings, choose some event you know you will be attending in the near future and take time to visualize it in your mind, seeing yourself the way you want to be – feeling confident and enjoying the company of others.

Imagery can also be used in a more symbolic way to work on general feelings of confidence, calmness and positivity. The following exercise presents a number of visualizations on this theme, including suggestions originating from the work of Stanton (The Cloud and The Lake[3]), Walch (The Balloon[4]) and Jackson (The Stream[5]). Experiment with them to find out what is useful for you. You may find that ideas for personal symbolic visualizations of your own flow quite readily. Be creative!

Exercise
Make yourself comfortable and close your eyes . . .

The Cloud

1 Imagine a big, white, fluffy cloud drifting and hovering above your head.
2 Like that cloud, allow your mind to gently drift and whenever anything which you feel has added to your lack of self-esteem comes into your mind (no matter how insignificant it appears to be) place it into that cloud.
3 Notice in time how that cloud increasingly darkens the more laden down it becomes. When you have reached a point where you feel you have placed into the cloud everything negative that comes to mind in this respect, observe the blackness of the cloud.
4 Now from behind the cloud notice a beam of sunshine. This sunlight can represent your determination to have that healthier, more positive sense of self that is rightfully yours.
5 As the light behind the cloud becomes increasingly strong and bright, watch with a sense of deep relief as the cloud burns away. Any obstacles to you having a positive self-esteem disappear with it.
6 With nothing left of the cloud or its contents you can now enjoy basking in the full warmth of the sunshine. You can allow that healing light to touch every part of you in time, increasing your sense of confidence in yourself and the brighter future that lies ahead.

The Tree

1 Imagine that your body is like a strong healthy tree.
2 Notice how the leaves seem to dance in the breeze in a carefree way.
3 The roots of the tree are deep in the ground holding you safe and steady. This can give you a sense of inner security as you continue to branch out further in your life.

The Room

1 Visualize yourself in a room which you are about to tidy out. There are big black bin bags beside you for any rubbish.
2 The deeper part of your mind can allow certain items in that place to represent the positive in your life, other items the negative (such as negative thoughts, feelings, beliefs or behaviours).
3 Just notice what items you feel drawn towards to dump into the bin bags. Consciously you need not know precisely what each item represents, except that the deeper part of your mind deems it appropriate, and to your benefit, that you be free of it.
4 Complete this visualization when you feel that the room is as you would like it to be for now.
5 Imagine dumping the filled black bin bags in a large dustbin which is then taken away.
6 There is now more space in the room for new items of your choice. You can allow these items to represent what you would like more of in your life, such as higher self-esteem, love, happiness and health.

The Lake

1 Visualize yourself standing at the side of a lake.
2 The part of this lake nearest to you is grey and dreary, the water windswept and rough.
3 The other side of the lake, however, looks very different. The waters are calm and reflect a blue sky above. There are people sitting there enjoying the sunshine and the beautiful scenery.

The atmosphere seems cheerful and uplifting. This is the shore of healthy self-esteem.

4 See yourself crossing this lake – you may be rowing a boat or even swimming.

5 Observe how, no matter what obstacles come your way (such as the wind and rough waters), you manage to overcome them. If you need to take any rests along the way you can make a short stop at one of the small islands dotted about the surface of the lake.

6 Finally, as you reach that brighter side you can allow yourself to become aware of an energizing feeling of confidence welling up within you. Take some time just to 'be' with that special place and feeling.

The Balloon

1 Imagine that you are strolling down a beautiful country lane. Allow relaxation to develop and increase with each step you take.

2 Enjoy and take interest in your surroundings by exploring them with all of your senses in your mind. Make them every bit as beautiful as you would like them to be.

3 Imagine that you are carrying a large pack on your back. As the lane leads you up a small hill, notice the dead weight of this pack. The heavy contents of the pack can represent unwanted negative feelings.

4 On reaching the top of the hill you find an open gate leading into a beautiful meadow. In the middle sits a large, colourful, hot air balloon with a big basket beneath it. Strong ropes hold the balloon down.

5 Walk over to the balloon and drop your heavy back pack to the ground. Open the pack and one by one take out its contents (representing those unwanted feelings) and place them in the basket. Notice how your negative feelings decrease with each object you put into the basket. Enjoy that process.

6 As soon as you have disposed of the last object from the pack you can become aware of a feeling of deep relief and peace inside.

7 Nearby on the grass you may notice a large knife or hatchet. Use this to cut the ropes and set the balloon and basket free.
8 Lie down on the comfortable, warm, soft grass and watch that balloon float away. As you do so, you can notice a feeling of further release and calm. As the balloon drifts further and further away, soon to be out of view, really enjoy that feeling of being free from those unwanted feelings.

The Stream

1 Visualize yourself sitting on the grassy bank of a stream, enjoying the shade of a large tree.
2 As you gaze into the clear water, you can allow yourself to feel soothed by the invigorating sounds as it swirls and gushes around the stones and rocks.
3 A gentle breeze rustles the leaves of the tree and from time to time some of them fall on the ground nearby.
4 Pick up one of those leaves. Imagine placing onto that leaf any negative beliefs, thoughts and feelings which you consider you will be better off without at this time.
5 Place the leaf gently onto the water and let it go.
6 Watch that leaf as it slowly drifts away, taking with it any barriers to a healthy self-esteem.
7 You can repeat this process with as many leaves as you feel may be appropriate.

Having completed your visualization/s, open your eyes feeling refreshed, calm, confident and alert.

We often find ourselves in testing situations where we could do with an extra boost of confidence, for example, while waiting to go into a job interview or when we are about to meet new people. Would it not be wonderful if you could 'call on' a feeling of confidence when you feel you most need it? The following technique, which is adapted from the work of Stein,[6] aims to help you do just that! It utilizes the mind's natural talent for linking things together and making associations.

Exercise

1 Close your eyes and allow yourself to feel comfortable.
2 Scan your memories and identify any time in your life when you felt confident and good about yourself.
3 Allow yourself to travel back to that experience. Visualize and re-live it in your mind, getting a sense of those feelings you felt then. Explore and enjoy that positive time once more in your mind.
4 When you can experience that confident feeling, close your dominant hand into a tight fist. As you do this, allow those feelings of confidence to increase. That fist can represent your inner strength and determination to be that more confident person.
5 As you clench your fist tighter still, allow that marvellous feeling of confidence to reach out and touch every part of you.
6 Repeatedly tell yourself that, in future, whenever you close your dominant hand into a tight fist in this way you can once again enjoy this feeling of confidence.
7 Relax and open that fist.
8 Before completing the exercise, make that hand into a fist of confidence once more and notice how that confident feeling can come flowing through.
9 Open your eyes feeling refreshed, confident and alert.

The more you practise this exercise, the stronger that association between clenching your fist and feeling confident can become. Knowing there is something you can do to instantly boost your confidence in any situation can in itself boost your confidence even further.

FULLY APPRECIATING YOURSELF

Because no one is perfect we all have our 'bad points' as well as our good ones. To be human is to have faults. When we have a poor self-image, we are prone to view ourselves more in terms of our faults than our good qualities. Rather than accepting our faults as part of who we are, we tend to be completely intolerant of them. We reject these parts of ourselves and in so doing we reject ourselves. This way of viewing ourselves prevents us from ever feeling 'whole'. It also means we will find it difficult to fully appreciate how special and lovable we are. We can feel particularly uncomfortable when others show us love and appreciation. Although we crave this kind of attention, we somehow do not believe we deserve it. We may think that we need to be 'perfect' before we can have the love and respect of others.

The following meditation is adapted from John Bradshaw's variation[7] of a technique originally conceived by Virginia Satir.[8] Towards the end of the exercise Shakti Gawain's influence is evident.[9] The aim of this exercise is to help you to acknowledge and become more accepting of all parts of yourself and to increase your capacity to be more open to the love and appreciation others show you. No matter how awkward or embarrassed you might feel throughout, stay with it! Give yourself about 30 minutes to really be with this work. Because there is a lot involved in this exercise it may help to have a therapist or trusted friend guide you through it.

Exercise
1 Close your eyes and allow yourself to feel comfortable.
2 Imagine yourself sitting in a front-row seat in a beautiful theatre. Allow it to be exactly the way you would like it to be. Notice the colours and the fabrics.
3 As the curtain opens you can allow yourself to feel the characteristic excitement such an occasion can bring. *The* [your name] *Parts Review* is clearly written across the back of the stage.
4 Take time to think of a part of yourself that you really like and imagine someone who could represent that part of you walking onto the stage. For example, if you feel you are

intelligent maybe you will see Einstein coming out. If you feel you have a good sense of humour you may like to see your favourite comedian walk on stage. Hear the audience cheer.

5 Repeat step 4 until you have five people standing on the right-hand side of the stage.

6 Now take time to think of a part of yourself you do not like and again see someone who can represent that part of you come out on the stage. For instance, if you feel you gossip about others you may choose to represent this part of you with a television character who is noted for being a gossip. Have this individual stand on the left-hand side of the stage. Hear the audience boo and hiss.

7 Repeat step 6 until you have five people standing on the left-hand side of the stage.

8 Now imagine a very wise person walking onto the stage and standing in the centre. When I am doing this exercise I tend to see this person as a wise old man similar in appearance to a picture of 'Merlin the Magician' which I saw many years ago in a children's book. Make your image of this wise individual personal to you.

9 This wise person invites you up onto the stage to re-evaluate these various parts of yourself (see figure 11). There on the stage take some time to look into the eyes of each of these people representing a part of you.

10 Focus on whatever issues you are dealing with in your life right now. As these different parts of you interact to cope with these issues allow yourself to reflect on the following for each part (negotiating with the wise person on the stage if this is helpful):

- Is this part in *direct* conflict with another part? (If the answer is 'yes', there is an exercise in the next section which will help you do even deeper work on this conflict.)
- What does the part have to say about your issues?
- Think of the possible benefits or positive purpose or intention of this part. (What would you lose if you did not have this part?)
- Think of the disadvantages of this part.
- What can this part teach you? (In particular, be aware of this question with parts of yourself you do not like.)

Figure 11 *The 'fully appreciating yourself' exercise*

- Would you like to change this part? If so, how would you modify it to enable it to be more beneficial to you? For instance, you may think of an alternative, more appropriate, behaviour it could generate instead of the present behaviour, which could serve the same positive purpose or intention of the present behaviour. If you do decide to change the behaviour of this part, double check that it feels better and right for you in this new way.
11 As you acknowledge that all of these parts make up the 'balance' within you, walk up to each part and allow yourself with love and acceptance to embrace it. Imagine each part melting into you in turn.
12 You may wish to thank the wise person for helping you before saying farewell for now. As he/she leaves the stage hear yourself saying to the audience before you, 'I accept and love every part of myself.'

13 Focus on one person in front of the stage (it can be someone you know or a stranger). Notice how they are looking at you with love and appreciation. Listen as they tell you something they really admire about you.
14 As you expand your awareness once more to incorporate a larger audience you can notice that they too are looking at you with admiration and respect in their eyes.
15 This audience now begin to clap and cheer before you. Feel the energy of love surging from them to you. Allow yourself to accept it into yourself. It may help to see the energy as a golden light, filling you up, healing every part of you.
16 Take a bow and thank everyone for making you feel the special person that you are.
17 Open your eyes feeling refreshed, confident and alert.

HANDLING INTERNAL CONFLICT

As highlighted in the previous section, we can have many 'parts' within us – some we like, some we may dislike. Sometimes parts of us can be directly in conflict, seeming to pull us in opposite directions. For example, as you work to enhance your self-esteem it may be that you need to take on board new, more positive, beliefs about yourself. The part of you engaged in the new way of thinking about yourself may come into direct conflict with the part of you viewing yourself 'the old way'. You may feel torn between these two parts of yourself, feeling uncomfortable no matter what you choose to believe about yourself at any one time because a part of you will raise an objection. As you can imagine, this could well impede your progress with improving your self-esteem! Inner conflict between opposing parts within us may require further more focused work in addition to that outlined in the previous section.

   The exercise at the end of this section, similar to that in the previous section, makes a very important assumption. It incorporates the notion that all parts of us have some positive purpose or intention regardless of how negative or destructive the behaviour it generates appears to be on the surface. (You may already have grasped some sense of this concept in the previous exercise when working with the parts of you that you dislike.) Usually, as human beings, we only engage in certain behaviour because at some level within ourselves we appreciate we are getting something out of it. Denise's story highlights this point and serves as a good background for the technique to follow.

Denise was a happily married woman. She stayed at home looking after the children and minding the house, more out of her belief that she had nothing to offer the job market than her desire to be a mother at home. Her husband liked having her there in the evenings when he got home from work. His job was very demanding and he found it really helpful to talk things through with her at the end of the day. He equally liked to hear about her day. Denise was pleased that he shared his worries with her and she always enjoyed these evening talks. It was 'their time' as a couple.

A friend of Denise's lent her a book on self-esteem and she began working on improving how she felt about herself. In time a part of Denise began to see herself very differently. As her confidence grew she decided to enrol on a business studies evening course with a view to subsequently working outside the home. At first her husband was very encouraging. However, it meant that two evenings a week on returning from work he had to feed the children and put them to bed. Afterwards, he would sit down on his own missing the company of his wife. Whenever she was at home the first chance she got she would lock herself away in another room to work on her assignments. She found herself excelling in her studies and became excited by the added confidence this gave her. Denise's husband began objecting strongly because they were spending less time together. They began to argue.

Over time, part of Denise started to experience self-doubt once more. This made it difficult to concentrate on her studies. She referred to this part of her as her 'self-destructive part' which was trying to wreck her chance to improve herself. Initially she could not see anything positive about it at all, but on deeper reflection she was able to appreciate that the positive intention or purpose of this part of her was to make her give more attention to her husband.

Denise's inner conflict is a familiar one. Many people have one part of them sensitive to the needs of others, and another part 'wanting to be themselves'. However, opposition arises only when we see these two objectives at opposite ends of the spectrum, which need not be the case. In Denise's situation, the part of her that appeared self-destructive and the part of her that was feeling confident and ambitious had at least one common purpose – both were working for something she valued (one for her marriage, the other for the chance of a career). Finding common ground between parts which initially appear to be in conflict is the first step towards calming the struggle within. The second step involves actively searching for alternative, more appropriate, ways to satisfy the positive purpose of the part which initially seems destructive or negative. In Denise's case, rather than taking the path of self-doubt and giving up her studies in order to have more time for her husband, she could decide instead, for example, to opt for a similar course running during the day when the children are at school. She could also decide to limit her study to set times, as negotiated between herself and her husband. This would both allow her to continue following her plans for a career and ensure that her husband did not feel neglected. It just goes to show, you can have your cake and eat it! It just needs a bit of work.

Most of us have some parts inside us that appear to be in conflict. The exercise that follows, often entitled the 'visual squash', can help us to become 'unstuck'. It is a simple yet powerful technique that helps to resolve the battle within.

As in the exercise in the previous section, it involves implementing more appropriate behaviours with the same positive purpose in place of destructive or negative behaviours. Accepting and valuing parts of you rather than rejecting any part of the self is also at the core of this work.

The technique in the exercise was initially developed by Richard Bandler and John Grinder,[10] founders of an approach known as 'Neuro-Linguistic Programming' (NLP). NLP deals with the way we structure our subjective experience in our minds. It has developed a series of models and ways of coding human behaviour to comprehend how people do what they do to create their own experience. The complicated title 'Neuro-Linguistic Programming' can be broken down as follows:

- *Neuro* refers to our physiological responses to concepts and events and the notion that behaviour stems from our neurological processes of sight, hearing, touch, smell and taste.
- *Linguistic* takes into account not only how we utilize language to communicate with others, but also the structuring of our thoughts and behaviour.
- *Programming* indicates that we have choice in how we organize our thoughts and behaviour to produce different results.

Exercise
1 Identify and separate the conflicting parts within you.
2 Find a way to represent each part. For instance, if there are two parts you may allow your hands to symbolize the parts. Develop an awareness of which hand is to stand for which part and hold them out in front of you, body width apart, palms facing.
3 Explore what the positive purpose or intention of each part might be. Ask each part in turn.
4 Emphasize how staying in conflict could mean neither part fully achieving its purpose. Negotiate with the parts to find

out what they have in common with respect to what they want to achieve for you. Speak to these parts in the same manner as you would to individuals. If they are adamant that they have nothing in common you can at least get them to agree on the fact that they both have an interest in your wellbeing and survival.

5 Get a sense of whether each part is willing to join forces and integrate with the other in order to work towards their common goals. It is not necessary for this to happen, but if they are willing to come together you can allow your hands to come together in their own time with as little conscious effort as possible. When they reach each other clasp them together (visually squash them).

6 Now with acceptance and love embrace the integrated parts into yourself – imagine them melting into you.

7 Observe how you feel inside now compared to when you began this exercise.

FREEING YOURSELF FROM ATTACHMENT TO OTHERS

In Chapter 2 the concept of fear of abandonment was outlined. If we are emotionally dependent on others this can result in fear of abandonment. The thought of losing people who provide us with something so essential to our wellbeing is very frightening. I was particularly dependent on my mother, even into my married life. I realized that not only was this unhealthy for me but it was also not doing my relationship with my husband Mark any favours. I used the powerful exercise presented in this section, which is adapted from the ideas of Connirae and Steve Andreas and Robert McDonald,[11] to help me to release my tendencies towards codependence and start building instead a healthier replacement – my own sense of self. It also in time allowed me to appreciate, respect and love my mother more as a person in her own right rather than as someone to meet my needs. I am really pleased I took the time to do this work.

As I have previously stated, my mother has passed away. She died of cancer over four years ago. I know I would have been even more devastated, perhaps totally lost, had I not addressed my attachment to her a number of years before. You will benefit from working through the following for about 15–20 minutes. (A summary of the exercise is outlined in figure 12.)

Exercise

1 Unlike the other exercises in this book where you are seated while carrying out your work, it is suggested that for this one you stand. Close your eyes to help you to focus internally.

2 Identify someone to whom you feel you may be attached – a parent or a spouse, for instance.

3 Imagine this person is standing near you. Study what he/she looks like. Reach out and touch the person if you wish. Really focus your attention on how you feel in the company of this person. Be particularly aware of your attachment to him/her.

4 Find a way to symbolize your attachment to this person. For example, to represent my connection with my mother, I visualized a cord linking my heart to hers. Clients have often described to me links with other parts of the person's body, such as the stomach or head. Experiment and find whatever representation feels appropriate to your situation.

5 Now take time to clarify for yourself what the positive purpose of such a connection with this person is. What does it do for you? It might be, for example, that it helps you to feel loved or safe.

6 Create a picture of yourself in your mind. Allow this image to be one of a more evolved and 'self-sufficient, developing you' who is able to provide the positive purpose of the attachment to the other person. This more resourceful you wants to be there for you, to love and care for you. Pay attention to everything about this image of you – how you sound as you speak, your posture, the way you are dressed, how it feels to touch this you.

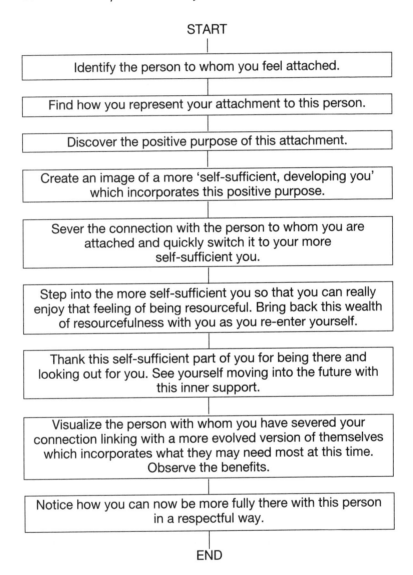

START

Identify the person to whom you feel attached.

Find how you represent your attachment to this person.

Discover the positive purpose of this attachment.

Create an image of a more 'self-sufficient, developing you' which incorporates this positive purpose.

Sever the connection with the person to whom you are attached and quickly switch it to your more self-sufficient you.

Step into the more self-sufficient you so that you can really enjoy that feeling of being resourceful. Bring back this wealth of resourcefulness with you as you re-enter yourself.

Thank this self-sufficient part of you for being there and looking out for you. See yourself moving into the future with this inner support.

Visualize the person with whom you have severed your connection linking with a more evolved version of themselves which incorporates what they may need most at this time. Observe the benefits.

Notice how you can now be more fully there with this person in a respectful way.

END

Figure 12 *Summary of the 'freeing yourself from attachment to others' exercise*

7 Now turn to the person to whom you are attached. Imagine once more the manner in which you represented this connection and sever it. Quickly switch the connection to your more resourceful you (in exactly the same way as you had been connected to this other person). For example, I saw myself cutting the cord linking me to my mother and then linking it to the heart of my more resourceful self.

8 Enjoy the feeling of being able to receive from yourself rather than depending on someone else. Take some time to step into this more evolved you so that you can really get a sense of that feeling. You can also become aware of what it feels like to give to yourself in this way. Re-enter yourself bringing with you this wealth of resourcefulness.

9 Thank this more fully developed you for being there as your friend and support, now and in the future, always looking out for you. Appreciate that you can always count on yourself. Imagine moving into the future with this strength within, allowing you to relate to others in a more beneficial way, both for them and for yourself.

10 Look back at the person with whom you have severed the connection. Visualize them linking with a more evolved version of themselves which has evolved beyond their current level of resourcefulness – a self which incorporates what they may need most at this time. Observe the benefits they can obtain as a result of such a connection.

11 Take some time now in your mind to be aware of how you can be more fully there with that person in a respectful way.

12 Open your eyes feeling refreshed, calm, alert and strong.

As noted in Chapter 2 when addressing the topic of addictions, it is often the case that we reach out to something other than another person to have our unfulfilled needs met. The exercise you have just completed can also be useful as part of the work for handling certain addictions. For example, let us say you feel you are addicted to and have an emotional relationship with food (that is, most of the time you are eating to distract yourself from reality and to comfort yourself rather than because you are hungry). In the previous exercise, you could represent in a symbolic way your connection with food rather than with a person. You could then work through the technique in the same way, leaving out steps 10 and 11. You could work to discover the positive purpose of your overeating and then transform the connection with food into a connection with your more self-sufficient self (which would incorporate this same positive purpose). Your more resourceful self could then be there in place of your overeating, nurturing you with the comfort you need into the future.

CHAPTER 7

Healing and Letting Go of the Past

We all cling to the past, and because we cling to the past we become unavailable to the present.

BHAGWAN SHREE RAJNEESH[1]

Throughout this book one theme in particular has shone through – the notion that past experiences are very influential in shaping our self-esteem. Until we heal the past it may continue to intrude on the present and future. This chapter focuses on how you can begin to unleash yourself from the ball and chain of past trauma and negative experiences and allow your work towards creating a positive future to flow that bit easier. It will firstly outline how you can begin the process of nurturing your 'inner child'. This will be followed by an exploration of ways in which you can alter the feelings associated with specific problematic memories. Finally, the manner in which you organize time in your mind and the possibilities of re-organizing this more to your advantage will be examined.

WORKING WITH YOUR 'INNER CHILD'

I do not know anyone who can say that they have had a perfect childhood. Many of us suffer throughout our lives because of neglect of our emotional needs in our early years. John Bradshaw suggests that as we reach adulthood the child continues to live in us, striving to satisfy these unmet needs. He states: 'I believe that this neglected, wounded inner child of the past is the major source of human misery. Until we reclaim and champion that child, he will continue to act out and contaminate our adult lives.'[2] For example, in Chapter 2, on the topic of fear of abandonment, you may remember what I wrote about a past client named Cathy. As a child she did not feel loved and accepted. She found in adulthood that she was sabotaging her relationships with an insatiable craving for love, affection and attention. Cathy reported continuously asking her present boyfriend if he loved her. She could never hear it enough. She was depending on relationships in the present to meet her childhood needs.

The more you can nurture yourself and meet your needs from within, the less you will feel the need to reach outside of yourself for environmental support. Working with your 'inner child' can be very powerful in this respect. The aim of regularly practising the following exercise is to help you to start becoming more and more self-sufficient and independent in life. Since it has the potential to provoke many emotions you may wish initially to work through it in the presence of a supportive, trusted friend or a therapist.

Exercise
1 Make yourself comfortable and close your eyes.
2 Imagine yourself as a small child. Allow yourself to become aware of the following:
   • your age
   • your general appearance and dress
   • your surroundings.
3 Notice your initial feeling as you see that child.
4 Introduce yourself to the child letting him/her know that you are here to help.
5 Ask the child what he/she really needs right now. Sometimes the child may act in a mistrusting, cautious and protective manner, not responding to your question. If this happens you could ask the child what you need to do in

order to be in a position to hear an answer. Reassure the child that you can be trusted.

6 Once you have heard the child's needs, validate them. Tell the child that you are in a position to really understand what he/she is talking about.

7 Work towards meeting the child's needs. For example, if the child needs attention you may talk and play with him/her for some time. You may take the child's hand in yours and/or hug that child. Do what feels right for you and take as much time as you need.

8 Decide in yourself that you will be committed to looking after and caring for this child from now on. Put aside a few minutes of each day for your meetings. Make a promise to the child that you will be there for him/her everyday of your life.

9 Ask the child if he/she wishes to come home with you. If the answer is yes, with the child's permission embrace him/her with love and acceptance. Really experience him/her as a part of you. If the answer is no, tell the child that although your meeting is over for now, you will see him/her again very soon. You might like to wave goodbye once you feel it is appropriate to leave.

10 As you walk away imagine you are in a beautiful place of your choosing and allow yourself to become absorbed in the calmness of it. For example, you may imagine you are on a beach. Notice all the different colours of the sea as it stretches all the way out to the horizon where it seems to meet the sky. Hear the soothing sound of the sea in your mind. Enjoy the warmth of the sunshine. Or you may imagine you are in a garden or the countryside. Become aware of what you can see around you there, such as trees and flowers – maybe getting a hint of the fragrance of those flowers in the air as you breathe its freshness into your lungs. Perhaps the sun is shining down in that place, allowing all the colours to become alive and vibrant. Hear the sounds in that place, like birds singing in the trees or bees humming in the flowers.

11 Wherever you have chosen to be, take time in that place to reflect on the benefits of meeting with your inner child.

12 Open your eyes feeling refreshed, calm and alert.

Reconnecting with your inner child has the potential to heal many hurts from childhood. This in turn can free you to be more tuned in to the playful and imaginative qualities of the child within you. The following exercise is designed to help you awaken positive 'childlike qualities' which you may have lost along the journey to adulthood. It is adapted from the work of Louise Hay.[3]

Exercise

1 Make yourself comfortable and close your eyes.
2 Visualize in your mind a very special room that you can fill with people you love.
3 Now imagine those people acting as children – excitedly and happily playing, running, skipping, dancing, shouting and laughing. See them expressing all that is so wonderful about being a child.
4 Allow yourself to enter this room. Feel the joyful welcome from the people there.
5 As the others ask you what games you would like to play, bring to mind some games you really enjoyed as a child.
6 Take some time in your mind to imagine the fun you and the others are having as you play these games. Really immerse yourself in what you are doing, allowing yourself to experience to the full that childhood feeling of exuberant joy. Give the child within you the chance to be all it ever wanted to be – free, happy, loved and safe.
7 Open your eyes feeling refreshed, happy and alert.

As you work on yourself you may wish to carry out some childhood 'fun activities' in reality as well as in your imagination. Until I had my child a year and a half ago I had forgotten how much fun it is to play! Decide to do at least one playful thing a day and notice how much more enjoyable life can be!

ALTERING YOUR FEELINGS ABOUT SPECIFIC PROBLEMATIC MEMORIES

A lot of us have negative memories which from time to time bother us but do not greatly interfere with our lives. For some people, however, certain negative memories of the past can influence how they feel about themselves on an ongoing basis. Whether you have memories that bother you only slightly or ones that have a more debilitating effect, you should find the techniques in this section useful.

The past is over and done with. It exists only in the way we choose to remember it in our minds. This is good news, since we can change memories and their effects. Some of you may be wondering whether it is wise to 'tamper' with beliefs gleaned from experience which has helped you to make decisions in life. However, memories are notoriously unreliable.

What is a memory? A memory is merely a record of the last time we remembered that memory. We are all aware of how over time memories can change and become inaccurate. Also, when the memory was initially formed it was only an interpretation of the situation at hand. Chapter 2 of this book emphasizes how we can be particularly talented when it comes to distorting reality. Is it not reasonable to ask whether it is correct to put an inflexible programme into our minds to govern the rest of our life on the basis of a few memories which were formed in this fashion?

'Reality' in our minds is what we create it to be. If some of that 'reality' has no rational basis and is making us feel bad about ourselves then it seems appropriate to work through it therapeutically, by acknowledging and then actively changing it. Because throughout this book the focus has been on heightening your awareness of and directly addressing issues which may be adversely affecting your self-esteem, you can know that you are not purely becoming involved in a process of avoidance (as discussed in Chapter 2).

The exercises in this and the subsequent section originate from the 'Neuro-Linguistic Programming' approach referred to in the previous chapter. If your memory is usually represented in your mind by one main image, the first exercise in this section will be appropriate. However, the second exercise will be more suitable if your memory is stored in the mind like a mental film, made up of many consecutive images. I would strongly advise that if the memory you wish to work on produces very intense negative feelings, you work on these techniques with the help of an experienced therapist.

Exercise
1 Decide on a memory you wish to work with. When thinking of the memory notice what image comes into your mind.
2 On a 'bad feelings' scale ranging from 1 to 10 (with 10 as the worst), think of the number that represents how bad you feel as you look at this image.
3 Make yourself comfortable and close your eyes. Allow yourself to become aware of that memory in your mind.
4 By making various alterations to that image, you can test which ones lessen or neutralize the negative feeling produced. If, for example, the image is in colour, try changing it to black and white. Note any resulting change in the feeling experienced while looking at the image in your mind in this new way. Open your eyes. If the feeling has improved take a note of this alteration.
5 You can now experiment with further manipulations, always returning the image to 'normal' before testing a new alteration. Remember to take note of any alterations which make that bad feeling better or neutralize it completely. The following elements of your memory image can all be changed.
   • *Distance:* push it further away or bring it closer.
   • *Clarity:* make it more blurred or more sharply focused.
   • *Sound:* put in extra sound (for example, nice music) or take out the sound. Experiment with the volume.

- *Perspective*: take yourself outside the image (dissociate) and look at yourself in the image from that perspective. Alternatively, be in the image (associate).
- *Humour*: for example, if there are other people in the memory, dress them up as clowns or replace their voices with those of cartoon characters. Be creative!

This list is not comprehensive. You may think of other alterations you can make until your experimentation has given you a number of alterations that help the negative feelings.

6 Now breathe slowly and deeply and view the memory, bringing together all the manipulations you noted that neutralize or improve that negative feeling. For instance, it may be that turning the image to black and white, pushing it away, softening the focus and dissociating yourself from the image neutralize the feeling. (If you still feel more negativity than you can comfortably handle, go back to the experimentation stage once again.)

7 See the image in this 'new' way in your mind five times in succession, opening your eyes after each viewing.

8 Now look at your 'old' way of remembering the memory (if your mind will allow you to!) and see if it now registers a lower number on the bad feeling scale. You should feel less negative than before, or, ideally, neutral about that memory. If not, go back to step 5.

A case illustration will give you an idea how this very useful technique can work in practice. I remember using this approach with a client named Josie who came to see me on the recommendation of her doctor. Her negative emotions appeared to be manifesting themselves in the form of 'a headache which never let go from morning to night – sheer misery and agony'. Josie could trace her symptoms back to a visit she had made to her sister-in-law a number of years before. This woman had bossed her about and constantly criticized her, making her feel very small. Josie's self-esteem was such that she took this treatment without any retaliation – 'I had to do everything I was told.'

Although Josie was now choosing to have minimal involvement with her sister-in-law, the memory of that particular visit was something that she saw over and over again in her mind. It was causing her to feel very bad about herself and was also affecting her sleep. She said she would like to have a way of 'putting it away', of 'letting go' of the negativity generated by the memory.

Josie followed the technique outlined in the previous exercise and visualized the memory in her mind (she had one main image for this). She then reported how bad she felt when viewing the memory. Quickly, I asked her to experiment with certain alterations and we took note of those that helped her to feel better about the memory.

When we put these positive manipulations of the memory together it resulted in Josie seeing her sister-in-law dressed as a clown and guffawing and behaving in a ridiculous manner with the voice of a cartoon character. In the background the comical theme music from the old Laurel and Hardy movies was playing. Josie reported: 'By practising this technique I was able to see my sister-in-law in a totally different light. I found as I responded to this work I began to relax. From there I went from strength to strength.' Coupled with other work outlined in this book, Josie in time began to feel better about herself and, interestingly, her headaches disappeared completely.

For those people whose memory is not represented effectively by one image, but rather, is stored in the mind like a mental film, being made up of many consecutive images, the following technique is appropriate.

Exercise
1 Decide on a memory you wish to work with.
2 As in the last exercise, select a number between 1 and 10 to represent how bad you feel about this memory (with 10 being as bad as it could feel).
3 Make yourself comfortable, close your eyes and imagine you are sitting in a cinema looking at a blank screen.

4 Now watch the memory on screen, starting at the point before the negative feelings begin. Hold that very first image on the screen and have it there in black and white. At the same time imagine that you are floating out of your body and up into the projection room of the cinema, so that you are looking at yourself in the cinema looking at yourself on the screen.

5 From the projection room push a button on the projector that allows the mental film to run. Watch it through from start to finish in black and white, from the perspective of the projection room. Hold the last picture of the memory on the screen.

6 Now jump from the projection room and float into that last picture of the memory on the screen. Turn the picture to colour and rewind the whole film backwards at top speed within one second.

7 Repeat steps 5 and 6 another five times.

8 Now float into your body sitting on the cinema seat and watch the film from start to finish in black and white. Breathe slowly and deeply, noting how much that initial number out of 10 has gone down. Experiment if necessary with any other alterations (see previous technique) to reduce or neutralize the negative feeling.

This technique is said to work by destroying the habitual pattern of the memory. By rewinding the film very quickly, there appears to be a confusion or deletion of the trigger function of the initial image of the sequence. Repeat the technique in the future if the immediate positive effect wears off.

TIMELINE WORK

Timeline work involves examining how our brain deals with time and whether it can be organized in our mind more to our advantage. This section will certainly be of interest to those who feel preoccupied with their past and have difficulty planning their future.

Discovering your personal timeline

How do you as an individual recognize events from the past, the present and the future in your mind – that is, how do you code time? The following exercise will be useful in helping you to determine this. It is often made easier with the help of an experienced practitioner, but see what you can manage by yourself.

Exercise

1 Think of eating a meal last week.

2 Think of eating a meal next week.

3 Now think of both these experiences together. How do you know which is which?

Many individuals will have some sort of picture for each event which they report sensing in different locations in 'space'. As illustrated in figure 13, the past is often perceived to the left of the person and the future to the right (with the present in front). There are, however, no set rules on this. There might also be disparities between these two images in terms of their size and distance, focus, brightness, colour and so on. If you are not aware of imagery, just notice the locations where you sense the experiences.

4 Now think about eating a meal at the following times (remembering specific meals is not necessary, but notice particularly the *locations* in space where you think about these meals):
  • ten years ago
  • five years ago
  • yesterday
  • right at this moment
  • tomorrow
  • in five years' time
  • in ten years' time.

5 Discover your timeline past, present and future by linking the locations in space of each of these experiences with an imaginary line. Get some sort of sense of all the other events from your past and future and fill in the line to make it complete.

Figure 13 *Coding time: past and future events imagined in different locations in 'space'*

Experimenting with changes to your timeline: help for those preoccupied with the past

Once you have a sense of your timeline, it can be useful to carry out experimental changes and notice how they feel. For example, if in the previous exercise you found yourself imagining events of your past in a location right in front of you then chances are the past is something you are predominantly aware of. It may be useful for you to move your past timeline over to the left or the right and check if this feels in any way more comfortable. If you wish to be more future oriented it may make sense to place your future timeline in the prime location previously occupied by your past timeline (once this feels right for you).

In line with the first exercise in the section of this chapter outlining work with problematic memories, you may also decide to experiment, for example, with size, colour and brightness. This can be done in such a way as to draw your mind away from the past timeline and towards the future timeline. You might, for instance, decide to make your future timeline events bigger, more colourful and brighter than those on the past timeline, to make them really attract your attention. *If you do not feel completely comfortable with any changes, be sure to undo them and go back to your initial way of sensing time.*

Take some space for yourself to experiment with these suggestions and further ideas of your own. Be creative!

CHAPTER 8

Taking it Further

The reality is that every human being is broken and vulnerable. How strange that we should ordinarily feel compelled to hide our wounds when we are all wounded! . . . At fifty I am still completing the process of learning how to ask for help . . .

M Scott Peck[1]

Through the course of working on yourself, it may be that you decide to see a practitioner for some extra support or to help with any areas you feel are too much for you to take on by yourself. This chapter will briefly explore some of the help available.

COUNSELLING AND PSYCHOTHERAPY

Clients are forever asking me, 'What are the differences between counselling and psychotherapy?' Interestingly, even within these professions there is a longstanding debate on whether counselling and psychotherapy are two words for the same activity or whether definite distinctions can be established between them. This becomes even more complicated by the fact that neither group can come to a universal agreement regarding a definition for the activity it practises.

Without an initial agreement on the meaning of these terms, it begs the question whether 'counselling' and 'psychotherapy' can be compared and contrasted at all!

However, this has not stopped people searching for differences. Many argue that the approaches are distinguished by the severity of the client's problems. Counselling is described as being the briefer treatment for less severely disturbed clients, with psychotherapy signifying a more long-term approach for more chronic and serious problems.

Regardless of whether you decide to visit someone who calls him- or herself a 'counsellor' or a practitioner using the label of 'psychotherapist', you might expect one, or a combination of both, of the following approaches in your sessions together. The first mainly involves listening with both empathy and understanding and requesting information and clarification which is aimed at helping you to gain insight into any problems. Offering solutions is not usually part of the picture. In the second, a more directive approach, sessions tend to be more structured with the practitioner working through a variety of psychological techniques with you.

A practitioner who is prepared to be flexible in his or her way of working may be in a better position to tailor sessions to your specific needs as an individual. Many people seeking help often not only wish to talk things through and feel they have been listened to and understood, but also want to be presented with some possibilities for change in the form of appropriate psychological techniques.

HYPNOTHERAPY

Hypnotherapy is categorized as a branch of psychotherapy. It employs the state of hypnosis as the therapeutic medium through which a variety of psychological techniques can be applied. Hypnosis can be defined as a state of intense physical and mental relaxation where the subject, although aware of immediate reality, experiences a sense of detachment from it. The focus of attention is usually internal and narrower than when fully alert. When in a trance you are not asleep; it is thought that you are somewhere in between being fully alert and asleep. Hypnosis is a naturally occurring state, similar to daydreaming.

In Chapter 4 I referred to the notion of the mind processing information both consciously and subconsciously. When in hypnosis, the subconscious mind is thought to become more attentive and receptive to therapy in the form of suggestions and imagery. Although there is less conscious participation in this state than when fully alert, you nevertheless remain completely in control at all times. While in a trance state you will not do anything you do not want to do. Only suggestions that you believe fall within your fundamental interests will be followed through into actual experience. However, even when we are not in hypnosis, persuasive people can sometimes fool or trick us into doing something that is not really to our benefit. In theory, the same could happen in the presence of an unscrupulous hypnotherapist. Although your chances of meeting someone like that are very small indeed, I would recommend as a general rule that you never allow an unqualified person to use hypnosis with you.

Hypnotic techniques offer plenty of choices for enhancing self-esteem. Many hypnotherapists pass a range of such techniques on to clients, teaching them self-hypnosis. This has the empowering effect of allowing them to continue working on themselves long after their sessions have come to an end.

FINDING A PRACTITIONER

You may wish for your doctor to refer you to a counsellor or therapist or you may wish to seek one out yourself. It is important to ensure that you find someone who is both genuine and professional. Practitioners' training can vary in its length and quality. I recommend you check out the following points:

- How long was their training and what qualifications do they hold?
- Are they registered, and if so with which organization?
- How long have they been practising?
- What is their policy on payment for sessions? (I would be a bit uneasy about a helper who charges for a set number of sessions in advance. It is not usually possible to gauge accurately how many sessions will be required at the outset.)
- Do they have experience of working on the problem area you wish to present to them?

The organizations listed at the back of this book will provide you with further information, and many can let you have a list of qualified practitioners in your area. In addition to ensuring that you feel confident about a helper's professional background, it is also important to the success of your work that you can relax and feel comfortable with this person.

CONCLUDING THOUGHTS

Whatever you can do or dream you can, Begin it. Boldness has genius, power and magic in it. BEGIN IT NOW.

J W von Goethe[2]

This book furnishes you with a range of different ways to work on yourself to help you improve your self-esteem. As noted in Chapter 3, it is important to realize that reading the book will not be enough in itself. Many of the techniques will require regular and consistent practice. Similarly, if you decide to visit a counsellor or therapist, change will only happen when you decide to start making it happen. Have the courage to move forward and take charge of your destiny. Know you are worth the effort. My very best wishes are with you on that adventure.

So often we move through life expending energy trying to get those around us to change. If we directed even a fraction of that energy into work on ourselves we would be more loving as human beings, since higher self-esteem results in a feeling of greater love for those around us. A world where individuals could truly value and respect themselves would be a world where people could care for others more fully. If the human race as a whole could commit itself to the concept of improving self-esteem we would experience a dramatic change in the quality of life on this planet of ours.

Notes

Introduction

1 W James, *The Energies of Men*, Longmans, Green & Co, New York, 1911

1 Exploring the Concept of Self-Esteem

1 R Johnson and D Swindley, *Creating Confidence. The Secrets of Self-Esteem*, Element Books, Shaftesbury, Dorset, 1994
2 C H Cooley, *Human Nature and the Social Order*, Scribners, New York, 1902
3 D Jehu, *Beyond Sexual Abuse. Therapy with Women Who Were Childhood Victims*, John Wiley, Chichester, 1988
4 G Lindenfield, *Self-Esteem*, Thorsons, London, 1995
5 For example, J W Hoelter, 'Fractorial Invariance and Self-Esteem: Reassessing Race and Sex Differences', *Social Forces*, 61, 1983
6 R M Crain, 'The Influence of Age, Race and Gender on Child and Adolescent Multidimensional Self-Concept', in B A Bracken (ed), *Handbook of Self-Concept. Developmental, Social and Clinical Considerations*, John Wiley, New York, 1996
7 In M Rosenberg, *Society and the Adolescent Self-Image*, Princeton University Press, New Jersey, 1965

2 Problems Associated with Low Self-Esteem

1 P Cleghorn, *The Secrets of Self-Esteem*, Vega, London, 2002
2 C R Rogers, *Client-Centered Therapy*, Houghton Mifflin, New York, 1951
3 Adapted from J C McCroskey, *An Introduction to Rhetorical Communication*, 5th edn, Prentice-Hall, New Jersey, 1986 (reproduced with permission)

3 Are You Ready to Change?

1 L Carroll, *Alice's Adventures in Wonderland*, Macmillan, London, 1980
2 S Jeffers, *Feel the Fear and Do it Anyway*, Arrow Books, London, 1987

4 Compliments and Criticism

1 K Keyes, *Handbook to Higher Consciousness*, 5th edn, Living Love Center, Kentucky, 1975
2 Adapted with permission from D D Burns, *The Feeling Good Handbook*, Plume, New York, 1990

5 Managing Your Anger

1 J Roberts, *The Nature of Personal Reality*, Prentice-Hall, New Jersey, 1974
2 W B Swann, J J Griffin, S C Predmore and B Gaines, 'The Cognitive-Affective Crossfire: When Self-Consistency Confronts Self-Enhancement', *Journal of Personality and Social Psychology*, 52, 1987
3 W Dryden, *Overcoming Anger – When Anger Helps and When it Hurts*, Sheldon Press, London, 1996
4 G Lindenfield, *Super Confidence*, Thorsons, London, 1989

5 Excerpted from *Creative Visualization*, S Gawain, © 1995. Reprinted with permission of New World Library, Novato, CA 94949

6 E Sheehan, 'A Guide to Hypnosis for the General Practitioner', *Members Reference Book*, The Royal College of General Practitioners, London, 1992

7 E Sheehan, "The Control of Pain with Hypnosis', *The Therapist*, Journal of the European Therapy Studies Institute, 2 (1), 1993

8 H E Stanton, *The Stress Factor*, Macdonald, London, 1983

9 E Sheehan, *Anxiety, Phobias and Panic Attacks*, Element Books, Shaftesbury, Dorset, 1996

10 Adapted with permission from B Jencks, 'Methods of Relaxed Breathing', in D C Hammond (ed), *Handbook of Hypnotic Suggestions and Metaphors*, American Society of Clinical Hypnosis, W W Norton, New York, 1990

6 Visualizations for a More Positive Future

1 J C Pearce, *The Magical Child*, Bantam Books, New York, 1977

2 E Sheehan, *Self-Hypnosis. Effective Techniques for Everyday Problems*, Element Books, Shaftesbury, Dorset, 1995

3 Adapted with permission from H E Stanton, 'Confidence Building', in D C Hammond (ed), *Handbook of Hypnotic Suggestions and Metaphors*, American Society of Clinical Hypnosis, W W Norton, New York, 1990

4 S L Walch, 'The Red Balloon Technique of Hypnotherapy: A Clinical Note', *International Journal of Clinical and Experimental Hypnosis*, 24 (1), 1976

5 A Jackson, *Stress Control Through Self-Hypnosis*, Piatkus, London, 1990

6 Adapted with permission from C Stein, 'The Clenched Fist Technique as a Hypnotic Procedure in Clinical

Psychotherapy', *American Journal of Clinical Hypnosis*, 6, 1963
7 In J Bradshaw, *Healing the Shame that Binds You*, Health Communications, Deerfield Beach, Florida, 1988
8 In V Satir, *Conjoint Family Therapy. Your Many Faces*, Science and Behavior, California, 1982
9 S Gawain, *Creative Visualization*, Bantam Books, New York, 1978
10 Adapted with permission from R Bandler and J Grinder, *Frogs into Princes*, Eden Grove, London, 1979
11 Adapted with permission from C and S Andreas, *Heart of the Mind*, Real People Press, Utah, 1989

7 Healing and Letting Go of the Past

1 IBS Rajneesh, *Roots and Wings. Talks on Zen*, Rajneesh Foundation, Poona, 1975
2 J Bradshaw, *Home Coming. Reclaiming and Championing Your Inner Child*, Piatkus, London, 1990
3 In L L Hay, *The Power Is Within You*, Eden Grove, London, 1991

8 Taking it Further

1 M Scott Peck, *The Different Drum*, Rider, London, 1986
2 J W von Goethe, trans. B Taylor, *Faust. A Tragedy*, Random House, New York, 1967

Further Reading

Bristow, W., *Coach Yourself To Confidence*, Thorsons, London, 2001.

Burns, D.D., *The Feeling Good Handbook*, Revised Edition, Plume, London, 1999.

Davies, P., *Total Confidence*, Piatkus, London, 2002.

Fennell, M.J.V,. *Overcoming Low Self-Esteem. A Self-Help Guide Using Cognitive-Behavioral Techniques*, Robinson, London, 2001.

Gawain, S., *Creative Visualization*, New World Library, Novato CA., 1995.

Matthews, A., *Being Happy! A Handbook To Greater Confidence And Security*, Media Masters, Singapore, 2001.

McDermot, I. & Shircore, I., *Manage Yourself, Manage Your Life. Vital NLP Techniques For Personal Well-Being And Professional Success*, Piatkus, London, 2000.

McGraw, PC, *Self-Matters. Creating Your Life From The Inside Out*, Simon & Schuster, London, 2002.

Peiffer, V., *Positive Thinking*, Thorsons, London, 2001.

Roet, B., *The Confidence To Be Yourself. How To Boost your Self-Esteem*, Piatkus, London, 2000.

Sheehan, E., *Health Essentials: Self-Hypnosis*, Vega Books, London, 2002.

Sheehan, E., *Anxiety, Phobias and Panic Attacks*, Vega Books, London, to be published August, 2002.

Useful Addresses

The following addresses are provided for information purposes only and do not necessarily constitute a recommendation.

Counselling, psychotherapy and hypnotherapy

INTERNATIONAL

The Israel Institute for NLP
16 Revivim Street
Tel-Aviv 69354, Israel

Israel Psychological
Association
PO Box 11497
Tel Aviv 61114, Israel

Israel Society of Clinical and
Experimental Hypnosis
Secretary:
Prof. Karl Fuchs
44 Hanassi Avenue
Haifa 34643, Israel

International Counselling
Centre
Kobe Kasai Hospital
11–15 Shinihara-kitamachi
3-Chome
Nada-Ku
Kobe 657, Japan

Japanese Psychological
Association
2–40–14–902 Hongo
Bunkyo-ku
Tokyo 113, Japan

Japanese Society of Hypnosis
c/o Hitoshi Kasai
Graduate School of
Education Center
University of Tsukub
3–29–1 Ohtsuka
Bunkyo-Ku
Tokyo 112, Japan

AUSTRALIA

Australian Institute of
Professional Counsellors
Locked Bag 15
Fortitude Valley

Queensland 4006

Australian Institute of Neuro-
Linguistic Programming
705 Logan Road
Greenslopes 4120

Australian Psychological
Society
PO Box 38
Flinders Lane Post Office
Melbourne
Victoria 8009

Australian Society of
Hypnosis
PO Box 5114
Alphington
Victoria 3078

CANADA

Canadian Guidance &
Counselling Association
116 Albert Street, Suite 702
Ottawa
Ontario K1P 5G3

Canadian Psychological
Association
141 Laurier Avenue West
Suite 702
Ottawa
Ontario K1P 5G3

Canadian Society of Hypnosis
(Alberta Division)
7027 Edgemont Drive
Calgary
Alberta T3A 2H9

NLP Centres of Canada
5375 Tree Crest Court
Mississauga
Ontario L5R 3Z6

Ontario Society of Clinical
Hypnosis
Secretary: Ms Patricia
Derraugh
200 St Clair Ave W
Suite 402
Toronto
Ontario M4V 1R1

EUROPE

Berufsverband
Oesterreichischer
Psychologen
Garnisongasse 1
A-1090 Vienna, Austria

Oesterreichische Gesellschaft
für Autogenes Training und
Allgemeine Psychotherapie
Secretary: Dr Erik Boles
Testarellogasse 31/13
A-1130 Vienna, Austria

Oesterrcichische Gesellschaft
für Wissenschaftliche,
Kleintenzentrierte
Psychotherapie
Gespraegsfuhrung
Marienstrasse 4
4020 Linz, Austria

OTZ NLP
Teyberg 1/19

A-1140 Vienna, Austria

Belgian Psychological
Society
Laboratoire de Psychologie
Experimentale
Université Libre de Bruxelles
117 Avenue A Buyl
1050 Bruxelles, Belgium

Francophone des Lingues de
Santé Mentale
Rue de Florence
B 1050 Bruxelles, Belgium

Info Geestelijke
Gezondheidszoprg
Kortrijksesteenweg 369
9000 Gent, Belgium

Institut Resources PNL
37 Bois Pirart
B-1320 Genval, Belgium

Vlaamse Vereniging voor
Autogene Training en
Hypnotherapy
Secretary: Dr Pieter Roosen
Gebroeders Verhaegenstr 13
2800 Mechelen, Belgium

Irish Association for
Counselling and Therapy
8 Cumberland Street
Dun Laoghaire
Co Dublin, Eire

Irish Society of Clinical and
Experimental Hypnosis
Secretary: Mr P G Gamble
59 McCurtain Street
Cork, Eire

Psychological Society of
Ireland
13 Adelaide Road
Dublin 2, Eire

Association des Conseillers
d'Orientation de France
6 bis rue Chenier
92130 Issy les Molineaux,
France

Société Franchise de
Psychologie
2832 rue Serpente
F-75006 Paris, France

Deutsche Gesellschaft für
Artzliche Hypnose und
Autogenes Training
Secretary: Frau Elke Koch
Oberforstbacherstrasse 416
D-5100 Aachen, Germany

Deutsche Gessellschaft für
Klinische und
Experimentelle Hypnose
Secretary: Dr Uwe
Gabert-Varga
Gerokstrasse 65
7000 Stuttgart 1, Germany

Federation of German
Psychological
Associations
Geschaftsstelle des BDP
Heilsbachstrasse 22–24
D-53123 Bonn, Germany

Gestalt Education Network
International
Institut für Gestalt-Bildung eV
Oberweg 54

D-60318 Frankfurt, Germany

NLP Ausbildungs-Institut
Rathausplatz 7
D-6915 Dossenheim, Germany

Associazionne Medica Italiana
  per lo Studio dell'Ipnosi
Secretary: Dr G Mosconi
Via Paisiello 28
20131 Milano, Italy

Centro Studi de Ipnosi Clinica
  e Psiocoterapie 'H
  Bernheim'
Secretary: Dr G Guantieri
Via Valverde 65
Verona 37122, Italy

Italian Association of NLP
Via Bandello 18
20123 Milano, Italy

Societa Italiana di
  Psicologia
Via Reggio Emilia 29
00198 Roma, Italy

Societa Italiana di Counselling
Via San Martino della
  Battaglia, no. 25
00185 Roma, Italy

Dutch Association of Clinical
  Counsellors
Korte Elixabethstraat 11
3511 Utrecht, Netherlands

Dutch Organization of
  Psychologists
N Maesstraat 120
1071 RH Amsterdam,

Netherlands

Nederlands Instituut van
  Psychologen
Postbus 9921
NL-1006 AP Amsterdam,
  Netherlands

Nederlandse Vereniging voor
  Hypnotherapie
Secretary: Dr Chr. Koopmans
PO Box 4085
3502 HB Utrecht, Netherlands

Interaction
PO Box 1266 Vika
N-0111 Oslo 1, Norway

Norsk Psykologforening
Storgata 10 A
0155 Oslo, Norway

Norwegian Society of Clinical
  and Experimental
  Hypnosis
Secretary: Dr Gunnar Rosen
The Pain Clinic
Bergen University Hospital
N-5021 Bergen, Norway

Association for Neuro-
  Linguistic Programming
Unit 14
Wrotham Business Park
Barnet
Herts EN5 4SZ, UK

British Association for
  Counselling &
  Psychotherapy
BACP House
15 St John's Business Park

Lutterworth LE17 4HB, UK

British Psychological
  Society
48 Princess Road East
Leicester LEI 7DR, UK

British Society of
  Experimental and Clinical
  Hypnosis
Secretary: Ann Williamson
Hollybank House
Lees Road
Mosston
Ashton-under-Lyne, OL5 0PL,
  UK

British Society of Medical and
  Dental Hypnosis
Secretary: Mrs Angela Morris
28 Dale Park Gardens
Cookridge
Leeds LS16 7PT, UK

National Council for
  Hypnotherapy
PO Box 421
Charwelton
Daventry NN11 1AS, UK

National Council of
  Psychotherapists
PO Box 7219
Heanor DE75 9AG, UK

Scottish Branch – British
  Society of Medical and
  Dental Hypnosis
PO Box 1007
Glasgow G31 2LY, UK

United Kingdom for

Psychotherapy
2nd Floor Edward House
2 Wakley Street
London EC1V 7LT, UK

NEW ZEALAND

New Zealand Association of
  Counsellors
PO Box 165
Hamilton 2015

New Zealand Psychological
  Society
PO Box 4092
Wellington

USA

American Counselling
  Association & Council for
  Accreditation of Counselling
5999 Stevenson Avenue
Alexandria
Virginia 22304

American Psychological
  Association
750 First Street
NE Washington DC
20002–4242

American Society of Clinical
  Hypnosis
140 North Bloomingdale Road
Bloomingdale
Illinois 60108

National Association of
Neuro-Linguistic
Programming
7126 Eastshea
Boulevard
3B Scottsdale
Arizona 85254

Society for Clinical and
Experimental Hypnosis
221 Rivermoor Street
Boston
Massachusetts 02132

Index